Plowshares to Bayonets . . . In the Defense of the Heartland

A History of the 27th Regiment Mississippi Infantry, CSA

**(Excerpts from the Civil War Memoirs and Diary of
1st Sergeant Robert Amos Jarman, Company K,
"Enfield Rifles," Aberdeen, Mississippi)**

Complied and Edited by
COL Charles W. L. Hall, Ph.D.

Harber's Weekly

War for Southern Independence

STATE OF MISSISSIPPI – 1860

RE: MISSISSIPPI IN THE CONFEDERACY

Order this book online at www.trafford.com
or email orders@trafford.com

Most Trafford titles are also available at major online book retailers.

Plowshares to bayonets-in the defense of the heartland: a history of the 27th Regiment Mississippi Infantry CSA: the Civil War memories and diary entries of 1st Sgt Robert Amos Jarman / complied and edited by COL Charles W.L. Hall, Ph.D.

Includes bibliographical references and index.

1. Confederate States of America. Army. Mississippi Infantry Regiment, 27th.
2. United States—History—Civil War, 1861-1865—Regimental histories.
3. Mississippi—History—Civil Wars, 1860-1865—Regimental histories.
4. United States—History—Civil War, 1861-1865—Personal narratives, Confederate.
5. Mississippi—History—Civil War, 1861-1865—Personal narratives.
6. Jarman, R.A. b. 1840—Diary.
7. Soldiers—Mississippi—Monroe County—Diary. I. Hall, Charles W.L., 1946-. II Titles.
    E546.S58 973.7462—' 00-00000

Printed in the United States of America.

ISBN: 978-1-4669-1280-9 (sc)
ISBN: 978-1-4669-1279-3 (e)

Trafford rev. 11/16/2012

 www.trafford.com

North America & International
toll-free: 1 888 232 4444 (USA & Canada)
phone: 250 383 6864 ♦ fax: 812 355 4082

PLOWSHARES

TO

BAYONETS . . .

IN

DEFENSE OF THE HEARTLAND!

Dedications

&

Memories . . . .

In preservation of my children's southern heritage.

and,

the challenge of my cousin Dale Greenwell, in his successful writing of the 3rd Mississippi Infantry;

In the memory of my dear friend, mentor, compatriot and scholar

The late

Major-General William D. McCain, US Army. Retired. Adjutant-in-Chief, Sons of Confederate Veterans;

and

My fellow friends & compatriots of the

27th Mississippi Infantry (Regt) (Vol) SCV Camp #1329
Hattiesburg, Mississippi
1974-1977;

The Confederate Veterans, ladies and children of **the Great State of Mississippi**.

and

In the memory of our beloved

Confederacy . . . !

HISTORY

OF THE

TWENTY-SEVENTH REGIMENT

MISSISSIPPI INFANTRY VOLUNTEERS

IN THE

WAR FOR SOUTHERN INDEPENDENCE

Complied and Edited By:

COL CHARLES W.L. HALL, Ph.D.
Confederate Historian

Jackson, Mississippi

This story is a memorial to the men,
and their yet untold story of devotion and sacrifice in
Following units:

Jones' Brigade
Andersons' Division
Hardee's II Corps;

Walthall's' Brigade
Withers' Division
Polk's I Corps;

Brantley's' Brigade
Andersons' Division
S. D. Lee's Corps;

ARMY OF PENSACOLA
Department of Alabama-West Florida
(Staging Area)

ARMY OF TENNESSEE, CSA
(Field Operations)

General Braxton Bragg
General John B. Hood
General Joseph E. Johnston

st National "Stars & Bars"

Traditional

3rd National

"REGIMENTAL COLORS with HONORS"
Twenty-Seventh Mississippi Infantry of Volunteers
14 January 1862-27 April 1865

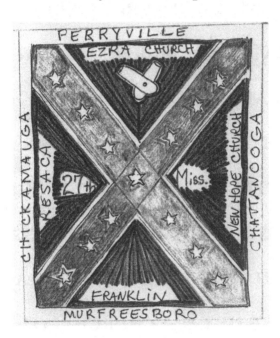

(The regimental colors were lost at Lookout Mountain)

Symbols of the Confederate Army in the Field
"Army of Tennessee"

"Polk's Corps"   **"The Battle Flag"**   **"Hardee's Corps"**

27th Regiment Mississippi Infantry Volunteers

Military Campaign Credits, 1861-1865:

I. BATTLE OF PERRYVILLE (KY)

II. BATTLE OF MURFREESBORO (TN)

III. BATTLE OF CHICKAMAUGA (GA)

IV. BATTLE OF LOOKOUT MOUNTAIN (TN)

V. BATTLE OF MISSIONARY RIDGE (TN)

VI. BATTLE OF KENNESAW MOUNTAIN (GA)

VII. BATTLE OF RESACA (GA)

VIII. BATTLE OF EZRA CHURCH—ATLANTA (GA)

IX. BATTLE OF NEW HOPE CHURCH—ATLANTA

X. BATTLE OF JONESBORO (GA)

XI BATTLE OF FRANKLIN (TN)

XII. BATTLE OF NASHVILLE (TN)

1862 Army of Tennessee	1863 Army of Tennessee	1864 Army of Tennessee
Hardees II—Corps	Polk's I-Corps	SD Lees II-Corps
Andersons Division	Withers' Division	Andersons' Division
Jones Brigade	Walthall's Brigade	Brantley's Brigade

TWENTY-SEVENTH REGIMENT MISSISSIPPI INFANTRY of VOLUNTEERS
Field and Staff—Headquarters, Pensacola, Florida

Colonel Thomas M. Jones (14Jan62), Commander***
*Lieutenant-Colonel James L. Autry (13Feb62)
*Major George H. Lipscomb (13Feb62)

COMPANY "A" "Oktibbenha Rifles"
*Captain E. Orville Huntley (8Jun61) Oktibbeha County

COMPANY "B" "Rosinheels"
*Captain A. Mc Lemore (10Aug61) Jones County

COMPANY "C" "Fredonia Hards"
*Captain Andrew J. Jones (25Jul61) Lincoln County

COMPANY "D" "Rayburn Rifles" Miss.Vols
*Captain E. R. Neilsons (28Aug61) Lincoln County

COMPANY "E" "Leake Guards / Rovers" Miss.Vols.
*Captain James A. Campbell (21Aug61) Leake County

COMPANY "F" "Covington Fencibles"
*Captain Hugh R. McLaurin (6May61) Covington County

COMPANY "G" "Kennedy Guards"
*Captain Julius B. Kennedy (17Sep61) Perry County

COMPANY "H" "Jasper Blues"
Captain Goodwyn Nixon (1Aug61) Jasper County**

COMPANY "I" "Jasper Rifles"
Captain A. J. Harris (20Sep61) Jasper County**

COMPANY "K" "Fifth Battalion/B"
Captain John B. Sale (27Sep61) Monroe County?

COMPANY "L" "The Twiggs Rifles"
*Captain H. B. Griffins (31Dec61) Jackson County

* killed	Transferred ***	resigned **

CONTENTS

PART TWO-The Valorous Defense . . . !!
THE GEORGIA CAMPAIGN

CHAPTER VIII.

CHAPTER IX.

CHAPTER X.

PART THREE-The Twilights last gleaming . . .
THE TENNESSEE RETREAT

CHAPTER XI.

CHAPTER XII.

CHAPTER XIII.

CHAPTER XIV.

CHAPTER XV.

CHAPTER XVI.

APPENDICIES

INTRODUCTION

There are no more survivors of the Twenty-Seventh Mississippi volunteers (the Regiment thereof). Their heroic deeds and adventurous exploits have been buried in the archives and libraries of last resort, much like the "volunteers in gray" who were interned along the dusty roads and byways across the battlefields of the Southern Confederacy, a legacy paved in victories, defeats, and finally in surrender! They returned home beaten and wore on the outside, but victorious on the inside from a higher morale plain of satisfaction—knowing that they had given there very best, and yet, they had served honorable, but in their mind they remained un-surrendered in their cause.

I the author have been interested in the War for Southern Independence since I was a young child, that interest was reinforced by the excitement of the Centennial 1960-1965, and finally brought to fruitarian through my own family's genealogical research. My interest in the Twenty-Seventh Regiment of Mississippi Volunteers (Infantry), was crystallized when the late President-Major General William D. McCain, University of Southern Mississippi, ask me to form a Son's of Confederate Veterans camp in Hattiesburg, Mississippi (a camp had not existed here since the 1950's).

At this time General McCain was serving also as the Adjutant-in-Chief, Son's of Confederate Veterans, headquartered at USM, and operated the Mississippi Division, Headquarters Camp #584 (of which I was a member in good standing since being credentialed in December 1972, while serving in the United States Army at Fort Ord, California).

I thought it a challenge and undertook to raise the Hattiesburg SCV Camp #1329. Prior to the actual chartering of the Camp, I had set about to learn our local history. I discovered that Forrest County had been derived from the Old Perry County. While researching the Confederate Archives at USM, further discovered that an infantry company had been organized of the men in Perry County of the City of Augusta. The unit was known as Company "G" and named the "Kennedy Guards," after their first elected commander—Captain Julius B. Kennedy on 17 September 1861, and accepted for state service.

During the month of January 1862, the Mississippi State Legislature passed an act, for the creation of Mississippi military forces. Early recruitment was under taken by the state militia and patriotic citizens. A new regiment would eventually formed from south-central counties of Perry, Jones, Leake, Covington, Jackson, Jasper, Monroe, Lincoln and Oktibbeha of Mississippi, and to be trained in camp at Brookhaven in the spring of '62. Company G—"Kennedy Guards" were ordered to Brookhaven, to become part of the new Twenty-Seventh Regiment, to be commanded by Colonel Thomas M. (Marshall) Jones, commissioned on January 14, 1862. Upon the initial organization of the regiment in camp, and the completion of area recruitment of nearly 1,050 men to fulfill personnel requirements of 10 infantry companies and regimental headquarters field & staff; training of the regiment could begin in earnest. The Twenty-seventh was mustered into Confederate Service, and ordered to Pensacola, Florida and transferred to the command of the Mobile Headquarters.

Upon the receipt of orders, the men and officers of the 27th Mississippi were jubilant and full of anticipation of the battle glory's to come—when they would finally met the "dam Yankee" on the field of contest and honor! The knew there patriotism and fidelity would lead to a triumph victory The regiments movement from Brookhaven, Mississippi was timely and occurred without incident, arriving in Mobile, Alabama for encampment. The regiment was detailed to coastal defensive and guard details in and around Pensacola, Florida.

During 1861 and early 1862, the war was well under way in Kentucky, Virginia, Missouri, Tennessee, and Louisiana. As of this time, the Confederacy had not as yet under taken any major campaign, the present emphasis was a war plan based on defensive posture—in other words waging a border war, buying time to muster available men and material from the interior states. The War and Naval Departments of the Confederacy needed time to develop war industries and procure all available arms and munitions from abroad. During this initial period they became aware that Gulf and Atlantic coastlines were relatively free of conquest, and the sea lanes were wide open for trade.

In mid-Summer, July 1862—the Twenty-Seventh Regiment of Mississippi was finally relieved of inaction; coastal defense and guard duties, and ordered to proceed in all do haste to join the Army of Mississippi, headquartered at Corinth, under the command of General Braxton Bragg (a Mexican War veteran officer). (The war was changing gears to a more aggressive stance and a cry to take the battle to the enemy up North). The regiment had been assigned to Hardee's Left Wing (Corps), Anderson's Second Division. The Regimental Commander, Colonel Jones had been promoted to Brigadier-General? And to command the Fourth Brigade (of Mississippi troops i.e., 27th, 30th, 34th and Lumsden Alabama Battery), while the senior field officer, Lieutenant-Colonel Autry took command of the regiment.

Major Operation Fall of 1862: A contest for the Border States. The major Confederate strategy was a three prong invasion of Central-Eastern Kentucky to secure Kentucky's admission to the Confederacy—in pronouncement of the states election to secede, and install its new Governor elect by the name of Johnston, at the state capitol in Frankfort.

The primary purpose of the invasion was secure enthusiastic recruits, and only secondly to check the federal army buildup-advance into the border state and the defenses of its major support base in Louisville at the falls of the Ohio River. Three confederate armies proceeded north: General Van Dorn's Army of Mississippi from Corinth, Mississippi through western Tennessee, into western Kentucky, objective: Bowling Green; General Bragg's Army of Central Kentucky from Chattanooga, Tennessee through central Tennessee, into central Kentucky, objective: Bardstown; and General Kirby Smith's Army of Eastern Tennessee from Knoxville, Tennessee through Cumberland, into eastern Kentucky, objective: Frankfort. After a number of early successes, the central prong of the Confederate advance under General Bragg was met by an over ambiguous federal army rush to Perryville on October 6th. Bragg's Army and the Twenty-seventh Mississippi would experience its first major combat action, between 7-8 October 1862 at the Battle of Perryville near the town of Perryville, Kentucky.

COL Charles W. L. Hall, PhD.
Confederate Historian

PART ONE

HURRAH FOR DIXIE...!

THE KENTUCKY INVASION

Twenty-Seventh goes to Camp . . .

CHAPTER I.

The STATE CAPITOL: JACKSON, MISSISSIPPI 1861.

On January 9th, 1861 the Mississippi State Legislature voted to approve "secession" and declared the Great State of Mississippi a "sovereign nation!" Colonel Jefferson Davis, commander of the veteran First Mississippi (Militia) Regiment, was ask to take command of the Army of Mississippi, with the rank of Major-General (and to date). General Davis worked tirelessly to organize Mississippi military forces. The first twelve infantry regiments had immediately been mustered, and organized into four state brigades. Shortly, thereafter, he was nominated to be the first (provisional) President of the new southern nation, then organizing in Montgomery, Alabama; to be known as the "Confederate States of America!" President Davis, being the new Commander-in-Chief, set about organizing all available military forces of the several southern states—as a military showdown in the field was on the horizon already. In other counties, like Perry and Monroe, they were buzzing with activity and preparations for the expected coming war!

RURAL TOWN: AUGUSTA, MISSISSIPPI 1861.

In Perry County, during the spring and summer of 1861 the war fever was running high! The men of the surrounding county met in Augusta, at the County Courthouse, and proposed the organization of a company under the leadership of Mr. Julius B. Kennedy, to be known as the "Kennedy Guards!" On September 17th, 1861, one hundred men were enlisted for three years or War and signed the muster rolls for the new unit under the supervision of Mr. J.B. Kennedy. The men meet and elected their officers: Julius B. Kennedy, Captain; J.B. Denham, First Lieutenant; John S. Byrd, to be Second Lieutenant; and John P. Carter to be First Sergeant. Shortly, the unit was ordered to march to Camp Brookhaven, Brookhaven, Mississippi for military instructions in battle drill, ceremonies, and bivouacing. 1

In late Fall 1861, General Samuel Cooper, A&IG, Confederate War Office (under the authority of the Confederate Secretary of War, the Honorable James A. Seddon, Richmond, Virginia) advised the Honorable John Pettus, Governor of Mississippi to send all available troops to the Department Commander, Alabama & West Florida, Headquartered at Mobile, Alabama for further organizing and equipping for Confederate Service. In December 1861, General Cooper ordered General Braxton Bragg, Commander, Army of Pensacola & Department, to organize an additional infantry regiment from ten infantry companies being transferred from the various counties in Mississippi, to be known as the "Twenty-Seventh" Mississippi. General Bragg had been furnished a list of recommended regimental officers. 1 4

CAMP BROOKHAVEN, MISSISSIPPI: Fall 1861.

Companies of the 27ᵗʰ Mississippi Infantry Regiment were organized separately between September and December, 1861 with men recruited in and from the counties of Covington, Jackson, Jasper, Jones, Lincoln, Leake, Monroe, Perry, Oktibbeha, and Simpson. 1

Later, they would become officially designated by the regiment as: Company A "Oktibbeha Rifles;" Company B "Rosin Heels," Company C "Fredonia Hards," Company D "Rayburn Rifles," Company E "Leake Guards," Company F "Covington Fencibles," Company G "Kennedy Guards," Company H "Jasper Blues," Company I "Harris Rebels," Company K "Enfield Rifles:" 1

RURAL TOWN: ABERDEEN, MISSISSIPPI 1861.

Company K "Enfield Rifles", (also known as Company B, Fifth Battalion Mississippi Infantry), locally known because it equipped itself with the Enfield pattern arm (of Cook & Brothers of New Orleans, for which the men paid $50 per short rifle with saber bayonet; purchased a total of 100 arms). The company was mustered into Confederate Service while camping at the Aberdeen Fairgrounds on September 27, 1861 by Lieutenant J. S. Lanier. After six weeks of camp instruction, were ordered to Mobile, Alabama on November 18, 1861. 1 3

Company L "Twiggs Rifles," (also known as the Griffin's Independent Company of Mississippi Volunteers) would be the final company to join the regiment—now complete. 1 3

After completing military instruction, the organized Mississippi companies were ordered by the state Adjutant General to march with equipment and provisions, and report to the Department Commander, Headquarters, Mobile, Alabama. 1

From Mississippi, to Mobile-Pensacola . . .

CHAPTER II.

PENSACOLA, FLORIDA: SEPTEMBER 1861

General Braxton Bragg wrote, on December 11, 1861 to the Secretary of War, "that a regiment of independent companies was on the eve of organization." Shortly thereafter, the War Department ordered Coopwoods's company to join Dowd's Regiment at Savannah, and instructed General Bragg to apply to the Governor of Mississippi for another company to fill the regiment." 2

On January 5, 1862, the Secretary of War wrote General Bragg, that President Davis "had recommended the appointment of Major Jones to be Colonel of the new regiment; and would be pleased to number the new regiment as the Twenty-Seventh; but that the President did not seem to entirely to concur in your recommendation of the Lieutenant-Colonel (Autry)." General Bragg in reply, urged the excellent service of the officer recommended and said: "I intend assigning this regiment, thus admirably officered, to Fort Rea and adjacent batteries."4 The Twenty-Seventh was assigned to the Army of Pensacola, Department of Alabama and West Florida, from January to March 1862. 2 3

By Mid-January 1861, all mustered companies and personnel, to include the Enfield Riflemen had arrival in Mobile and been designated a letter company of the new regiment, and quartered at old Camp Beulah. 2 3

By Mid-January 1861, a "Commissioning & Presentation Review" was ordered for 14 January. The regimental bugler sounded assembly, and all companies formed; reviewing officer's gathered at parade center; the post adjutant center field, called the companies to attention; then proceeded with the unit roll call: Company A, Capt. Huntley—All present! Company B, Capt, McLemore—All present! Company C, Capt. Jones—All present! Company D, Capt. Neilson—All present! Company E, Capt. Campbell—All present! Company F, Capt. McLaurin—All present! Company G, Capt. Kennedy—All present! Company H, Capt. Nixon—All present! Company I, Capt. Harris—All present! Company K, Capt. Sales—All present! And Company L, Capt. Griffin—All present! The post adjutant reports to General Bragg, Salutes, and says" All present and accounted for, Sir!" The adjutant then reads the first general order of the day, "Attention to Orders: Ordered by the War Department, Richmond, Virginia; Major Thomas Marshall Jones is hereby promoted to the grade of Colonel, PACS this date, by the Secretary of War, the Honorable James A. Seddon! An exchange of salutes between General Bragg and Colonel Jones. 1

The adjutant then read again, "Attention to Orders! Ordered by the War Department, Richmond, Virginia; All Companies and Personnel Assigned shall constitute the newly organized Twenty-Seventh Mississippi Infantry Regiment of Volunteers, this date, with Colonel Thomas M. Jones commanding, by the Secretary of War, the Honorable James A. Seddon! Salutes exchanged. 1

Following orders, Colonel Jones presented the regiment staff: Lieutenant-Colonel James L. Autry; Major George H. Lipscomb; Adjutant Crump; Surgeon Shelby; Assistant Surgeon Buckner; Quartermaster Craft; Commissariat Boyles, and Sergeant-Major Carter. General Bragg presented the regimental colors to Colonel Jones. 1 2

The new regiment now marched and passed in review of its commanders, with honor guard leading—carrying the new colors. Now, the regiment was fully ready for military service.

The regiment was assigned responsibility for general guard details until February 12, 1862, then were ordered to Pensacola, Florida to do general picket and guard duty, and to manage some coastal batteries between Warrenton navy yard and old Fort Barrancas. 3

While Company K was stationed at the navy yard, they "had good and comfortable quarters, and every convenience in the way of water, kitchen, etc., but the fleas were our great pest by night and day; but we had fresh fish whenever we wanted them, either by seine or hook and line. On one occasion we caught enough at one haul of the seine to feed three regiments and a battalion, and had remaining over more than would fill a common two-horse wagon bed. While there, a schooner run the blockade at the month of Period river, and had to be dismantled and burned to prevent it from falling into the hands of the Yankees, and among her stores were a lot of old rusty muskets, medicine and a considerable lot of rum which had to be hauled on wagons to Pensacola, and one night at the wagon yard, Burton, a servant of Dan Willis, discovered that the wagon master and teamsters had stolen and hidden in the sand under a house, a barrel of the rum. So next day, he "gave it away," and five or six of the men got a cart and horse from a Dago on the island and went to the wagon yard and captured the prize and brought it to the navy yard and put it in a closet just in rear of a building in which company officers were quartered, and drew it only at night, a I assure you they a gay old time while it lasted. Every morning at roll call it smelled very strong, Capt. John B. Sales would lecture them about it—they only let him smell "but nary a taste" did he ever get. During our stay in the navy yard the company was reorganized for the war and Capt, Sale was again elected." 3

Upon the departure of the Army of Pensacola for Corinth, Mississippi, Colonel Jones was assigned to command at Pensacola on March 9, 1862, was ordered to prepare for evacuation after the dismantling of the coastal installations. The regiment continued to be assigned to Department of Alabama and West Florida, from March to May 9, when the regiment marched out for Mobile; Company K remained till May 12th 1862 with duty at Fort McRae, Fort Barrancas, coastal batteries, and the Warrenton navy yard. 2 The regiment was notified of its upcoming movement and the decision to abandon the coastal installations. The regiment was given the task of striping the facilities of heavy guns, equipment, and stores for shipment to fortifications in Mobile and Vicksburg. Upon orders to depart for Mobile, the facilities at Fort McRae (commanded by Capt. J. H. Nelson), Warrenton navy yard (commanded by Major W. H. Kilpatrick, Fifth Battalion) and Fort Barrancas were destroyed by the Cavalry detachment commanded by Capt. A. J. Hays at 11:30 p.m. on May 12th 1862 by firing planted ordnance3, while under fire by Fort Pickens. 3 4

Company K arrived in Mobile at night on May 13, 1862 and "quartered in the old cotton warehourse. The following day, the unit joined the regiment back in their old quarters at Camp Beulah, four miles out on Spring Hill road, and on the land of Major Evans, the father of Mrs. Augusta Evans Wilson, the authoress of Beulah, etc." 3 For the next two months, the regiment would continue to train and make preparations, and gather provisions for the forth coming campaign. During this time the regiment was assigned to District of the Gulf, Department #2. 2 In preparation for the movement north, the regiment was assigned to Jackson's Brigade, Wither's Division, Army of Mississippi within Department #2 until August 1862. 2 Later, realigned with the Right Wing of the Army before the campaign. 2 3

Topical live in the Twenty-seventh regiment while stationed in Mobile, was narrated by the Orderly Sergeant, R. A. Jarman. He wrote "in May 1862, for a few days, we did guard duty around the city and over a lot East Tennessee bridge burners; then we put to work on the fortifications southwest of the city, at the old race course, and given our first lesson in earth works. About the first week of June we were moved south of Mobile, near the bay and near the Shell road just below the first toll gate. Some of the companies were put on the batteries out in the bay and others had charge of the shore batteries. Company K's battery was near camp and just north of the first toll gate, near Mr. Smith's (I think)? We had a fine time bathing after dark, for we were not permitted to go in during the day time on account of travel on the Shell road. Company drill and guard mounting in the morning; battalion drill in the evening at the race course by our then Lieutenant-colonel Hayes, of the regular army. He had before the war belonged to the United States Marine Corps; he was a fine officer and gentlemen and well liked by the regiment. Our Col. Jones was at Department Headquarters (in Mobile) at this time and we knew very little of him. While in the camp we had a race in each company at guard mounting each morning to see who would be excused from guard duty for a clean gun, for the man with the cleanest gun in company detail was excused from duty while the detail was on guard. I have known Jesse Carroll, now living in the neighborhood of old Camargo to wrap his gun in his blanket and sleep with it to get released from guard duty next day, and he would generally succeed, for his gun shone like a silver dollar. I, on one occasion carried off the prize, but only a week before I was marched out in the dirty gun squad to the Colonel, but was let off as I had been the day before at work on the earthworks and my mess had let my gun get out of tent, in the ditch, and full of sand during the rain, upon promise never to come up in the dirty gun squad again, which I never did; but I never but once came to the front with the cleanest. While we were camped here, Capt. Sale allowed Mr. W. M. Ogburn to put in a substitute, one Geo. W. Smith, and several others made like attempts, but all failed which caused some dissatisfaction. The favorite pastime of the men during the day was a game of marbles under several large live oaks along the color line of the encampment where we collected during the heat of the day. Here we enlisted Geo. O. Warner and B. H. Booth. The first recruit became to be known as a general clerk at the Headquarters of the Army of Tennessee, (which position was secured to him by Capt. Sale), and the latter was one of the main men in the Signal Corps of the Army of Tennessee." 3

While we were here, there was a proposition made for the man to give up their guns and change our organization from infantry to artillery and to be known as the first Mississippi Artillery, and to remain in charge of the batteries we had here erected; but some of the men, I might say the great majority, hooted at the idea, and said the war would soon be over and they would not get into the fight; but I tell; you they regretted their choice, for they did get fighting to their heart's content. 3

CHATTANOONGA, TENNESSEE: JULY 1862.

The men of Company K departed Mobile on July 22 by rail cars. It was reported that they were en route for three to four days. It was noted that during this time, Major Lipscomb of Columbus, Mississippi joined the regiment. Upon arrival in Chattanooga, the regiment proceeded to Shell Mound at Bridgeport, Alabama to do picket duty along the Tennessee River for about a mouth. [As the regiment prepared to rejoin the Army for the Kentucky Campaign in Fall 1862, we were put into a brigade which afterwards became known as Walthall's brigade, composed of the 24th, 27th, 29th, 30th and 34th Mississippi regiments;]. 3

General Bragg's army was transferred from Mississippi to Chattanooga for advance into Kentucky, the Twenty-seventh regiment was ordered to Chattanooga, where, in the re-organization of August 18, 1862, it was assigned to Hardee's Corps, of the newly created "Army of Tennessee." Colonel Jones was temporarily placed in command of Patton Anderson's Division, Left Wing of the Army, which included the regiment; Lieutenant-colonel Autry upon his return (having had been detailed to Vicksburg from March to July 1862) took command of the regiment. 3

In late August 1862, Bragg's army marched across Walden's Ridge and through middle Tennessee and reached Glasgow, Kentucky on September 13. Three days later they Chalmers Brigade attacked Munfordville and was repulsed, preparing to attack again and being outnumbered the federal army garrison finally surrendered. Hardee's Corps being in the advanced column entered Perryville. Aware that the federal army would be blocking further advance, both armies prepared for battle on October 8.

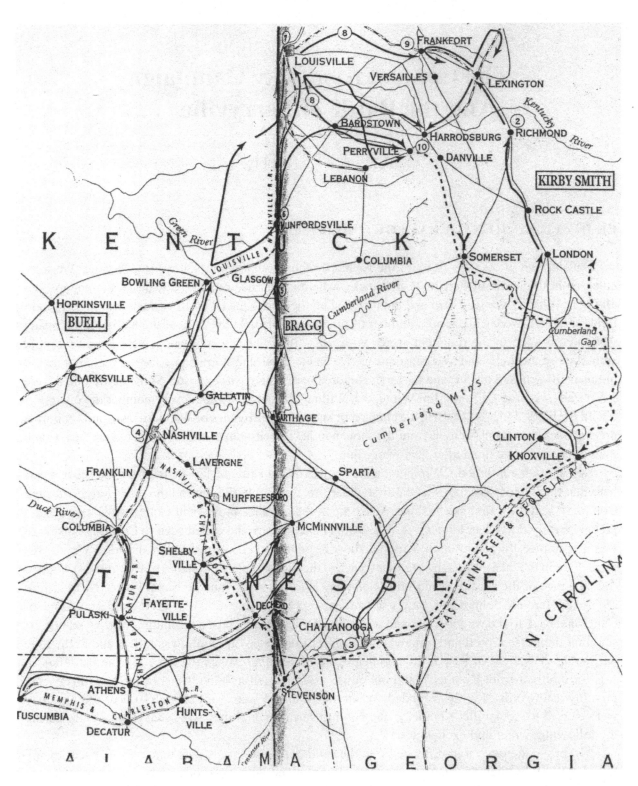

RE: THE CIVIL WAR OF THE WESTERN THEATER

The Central Kentucky Campaign
And the Battle of Perryville . . .

CHAPTER III.

PERRYVILLE, KENTUCKY: 8 OCTOBER 1862

Sgt. Jarman wrote "the fruits of the Kentucky campaign are now known to everyone. We were engaged in the battle of Perryville, Kentucky, where we burned our first powder at the enemy, and all the novelty of war was seen and the men had all the wire edge taken from them thoroughly, and I think about ten were killed and a number of others wounded. At the time of the battle our company was the only one in the regiment armed with rifles, the other ten companies were armed with old smooth bore muskets, and as a consequence we bad to do all the skirmishing for the regiment, and it put us in all exposed places, and under fire before the regiment was exposed. Some of the killed were J.A. Grady, George Lagrone, Jim White, S.J. Willoughby, and I cannot now remember the others." 3

In the battle Jones's (4th) Brigade charged in line with the brigades of Wood, Brown, and Cleburne, driving back the enemy in their front for about a mile. The casualties, however, were very heavy, and the victory did not extend along the whole line.

Sgt. Jarman continued, "While upon the subject of the battle of Perryville, I will say that it was here that the 27th Mississippi was the first under fire, and nobly did it stand the test. Here it was that Company K did its first skirmishing. While upon the advance movement Company K arrived at a precipice fully thirty feet high. Capt. Sale halted the company and called back to Col. Hays that here was a precipice thirty feet high. Colonel Hays responded, "Forward the skirmishers!" Which was done, Sale in the mist. When the regiment reached the place Capt. McLemore, of Company B, slipped over the face of the precipice and said "Company B follows me!" and he was followed by the entire regiment. Here old John, Capt. Sale's servant, was so badly scared that he ran the old gray horse of Capt. Sale back to the wagon train, and when the next day he received a scolding for riding so fast, he said that the horse scared and run away with him. Here Major Lipscomb was killed, and at the time he was the only field officer of the regiment from Mississippi. When the army left the battlefield it was for a retreat from Kentucky, and our entire wounded fell into the hands of the Federals except possibly a few only slightly wounded. When the wounded were well enough to bear moving they were carried to Louisville, Kentucky, and put into barracks until they were sent to Vicksburg during the following winter and exchanged." 3

"To prove the devotion of the negro to the southern cause, I will state that a servant sent by my father and my brother, J.E. Jarman, and myself, remained with my brother who was wounded here through the right shoulder, and brother Edgar said, that never was a man more faithful to any one that Isom was to him; washing and attending to him generally, and while in the barracks at Louisville he was not allowed to see him except at night, but then he always brought some tempting and appetizing morsel from the garrison officers, although before that he had been known to go without his meals all day rather than eat what the boys had picked up in their foraging trips." 3

It was reported that the Army of Tennessee fell back to Cumberland Gap, through which the troops passed October 19-24, retreating to East Tennessee. 4 The "objective point was Knoxville (by way of the Crab Orchard), and when the army reached there, the regiment was a dirty and smoked condition and very tired, and very glad of the few days rest received there and in the neighborhood. There the men enjoyed the luxuries of fine winter apples that they found in the country while foraging for feed of the teams; and pumpkin pies without shortening in the crust were brought to the camp and sold by the old men and women of the country." 3

"We moved from here to Chattanooga and Bridgeport, Alabama, by cars, and after remaining at Bridgeport a few days, moved to a place near Estelle Springs, on the Nashville & Chattanooga railroad, by rail. On the trip from Bridgeport the writer and some five or six other men went out to gather walnuts near the east end of the railroad tunnel under Cumberland Mountain while the engine pulled the train out and left them to walk through the tunnel, and I tell you, two men abreast made it so dark in there you could almost feel it. That night, we boarded the train with the second section of our regiment and rejoined the company just before daylight." 3

"Our next move was near Shelbyville; from there to Eagleville; from Eagleville to Murfreesboro. On all our marches here we found plenty of walnuts and hickory nuts, for they abounded all through Middle Tennessee. While at Eagleville or Murfreesboro, Lieutenant-colonel Hays was relieved from our regiment and Lieutenant-colonel Autery, of Vicksburg or Natchez, was **assigned** to duty with us." According to the reports, Colonel Hays was transferred to General Bragg's staff to serve as Inspector-General of the army. 4 "At about the same time we left Knoxville, or soon after Capt. Sale, of Company K, was promoted to the rank of Colonel of cavalry and detailed to serve as Judge Advocate at Army Headquarters, and Lieutenant W.H. Saunders promoted to Captain." 3 During this period, the 27th Mississippi of Jones's Brigade was assigned to Anderson's Division, 2nd Corps of the army from November to December 1862. 2

In November, Jones's Brigade included the Twenty-seventh, Thirtieth and Thirty-fourth regiments. Anderson's Division was broken up, and the Twenty-seventh and Thirtieth were joined with the Twenty-ninth and (?) regiments to form Anderson's brigade to be commanded by Colonel Walthall, in Withers's (Hindman's) Division of Polk's 1st Corps. This alignment would continue until September 1863. Colonel Walthall announced his staff on December 4, 1862. He was soon commissioned Brigadier-General. Just before the battle of Murfreesboro, December 1862, General Walthall being absent sick; Colonel Jones was in command of the brigade. 2 4

In December, the brigade then advanced from Chattanooga to Murfreesboro, Tennessee. 4

ORDER OF BATTLE CONFEDERATE FORCES			
CENTRAL KENTUCKY CAMPAIGN - BATTLE OF PERRYVILLE			
OCTOBER 7-8, 1862			
ARMY OF MISSISSSIPPI - C.S.A.			
Commanding: General Braxton Bragg			
15,000 Men			
RIGHT WING:			
Commanding: Maj.Gen. Leonidas Polk			
	FIRST DIVISION:		
	Commanding: Maj.Gen. Benjamin F. Cheatham		
		1st BRIGADE:	
		Commanding: Brig.Gen. Daniel S. Donelson	
			8th Tennessee
			15th Tennessee
			16th Tennessee
			38th Tennessee
			51st Tennessee
			Carnes Tn Btry
		2nd BRIGADE:	
		Commanding: Brig.Gen. Alexander P. Stewart	
			4th Tennessee
			5th Tennessee
			24th Tennessee
			31st Tennessee
			33rd Tennessee
			Standfort Ms Btry
		3rd BRIGADE:	
		Commanding: Brig.Gen. George Maney	
			41st Georgia
			1st Tennessee
			6th Tennessee
			9th Tennessee
			27th Tennessee
			Turner Ms Btry
		4th BRIGADE:	
		Commanding: Col. Preston Smith	
			3rd Tennessee (Escort) Cav.

			12th Tennessee
			13th Tennessee
			47th Tennessee
			154th Tennessee
			9th Texas
			Martin Fla Arty
LEFT WING:			
Commanding: Maj.Gen. William Hardee			
	SECOND DIVISION:		
	Commanding: Brig.Gen. James Patton Anderson		
		1st BRIDAGE:	
		Commanding: Brig.Gen. John Calvin Brown	
			1st Florida
			3rd Florida
			41st Mississippi
			A Btry/14th Georgia Bn-Palmer
		2nd BRIGADE:	
		Commanding: Brig.Gen. Daniel Adams	
			14th La Bn-Sharpshooters
			13th Louisiana
			16th Louisiana
			20th Louisiana
			25th Louisiana
			5th Btry-Co Washington Atry Slocomb
		3th BRIGADE:	
		Commanding: Col. Samuel Powell	
			45th Alabama
			1st Arkansas
			24th Mississippi
			29th Tennessee
			Barrett Mo Btry
		4th BRIGADE:	
		Commanding: Brig.Gen. Thomas Marshall Jones	
			27th Mississippi
			30th Mississippi
			34th Mississippi
			Lunsden Al Btry

	THIRD DIVISION:		
	Commanding: Maj.Gen. Simon Buckner		
		1st BRIGADE:	
		Commanding: Brig.Gen. Saint John Liddell	
			2nd Arkansas
			5th Arkansas
			6th Arkansas
			7th Arkansas
			8th Arkansas
			Swett Ms Btry
		2nd BRIGADE:	
		Commanding: Brig.Gen. Patrick Cleburne	
			2nd Tennessee
			35th Tennessee
			48th Tennessee
			13/15 Arkansas Cons.
			Carlton Tx-Sharpshooters
			Calvert Ark Btry
		3rd BRIGADE:	
		Commanding: Brig.Gen. Bushrod Johnson	
			5th Confederate
			17th Tennessee
			23rd Tennessee
			25th Tennessee
			37th Tennessee
			44th Tennessee
			Darden Ms Btry
		4th BRIGADE:	
		Commanding: Brig.Gen. Sterling Wood	
			16th Alabama
			32rd Mississippi
			33rd Alabama
			45th Mississippi
			15th Ms Bn-Sharpshooters
			Semple Al Btry
	CAVALRY DIVISION:		
		1st Cav. BRIGADE:	
		Commanding: Col. John Wharton	

			1st Kentucky (3Cos)
			4th Tennessee
			8th Texas
			2nd Georgia (5Cos)
			Davis Tn Bn (4Cos)
		2nd Cav. BRIGADE:	
		Commanding: Col. Joseph Wheeler	
			1st Alabama
			3rd Alabama
			6th Confederate
			8th Confederate
			2nd Ga Bn (5Cos)
			3rd Georgia (2-3Cos)
			1st Kentucky (6Cos)
			Bennett Bn
			12th Tn Bn (4Cos)
			6th Kentucky (2-3Cos)
			Ga Cav Bn-Smith Legion
Re: Bush, Bryan S., The Civil War Battles of the Western Theater; 1998; Pgs 35-36.			

PERRYVILLE, KENTUCKY 1862

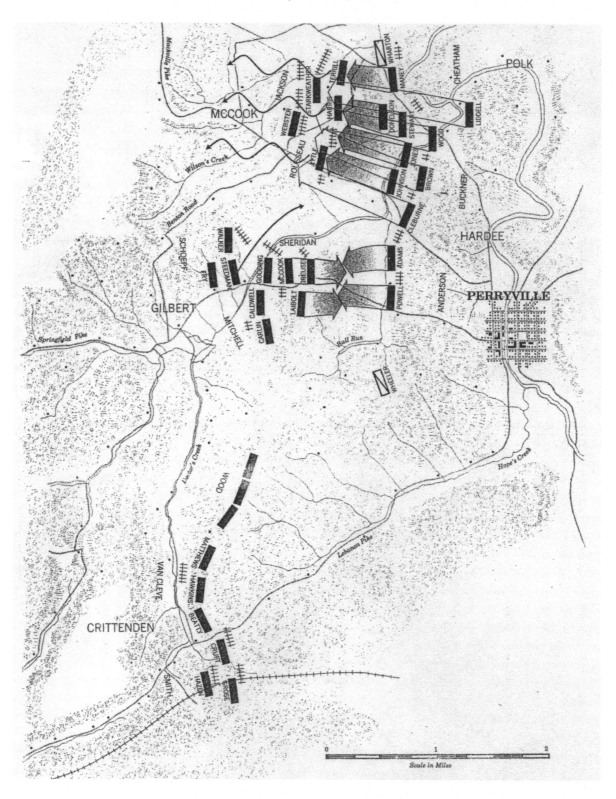

RE: ILLUSTRATED ATLAS OF THE CIVIL WAR
M

The Central Tennessee Campaign and the Battle for Murfreesboro . . .

CHAPTER IV.

MURFREESBORO, TENNESSEE: 31 DECEMBER 1862

Sgt. Jarman confirms "At the battle of Murfreesboro we again lost heavily as we were again the only company to do the skirmishing, although another company relieved us at night. We were at the front all day for three days before the battle, and in a thicket to the right of the turnpike that was so thick with vines and undergrowth we could scarcely walk through it. After the battle one could run through it and not stumble, so raked was it by the enemy's cannon. Here at Murfreesboro, Cosby, Hollis and J.B. Townsend were among the killed on the company and Henry Bradford among the wounded (I do not know remember all of those wounded or killed). Bradford's wound was from a canister shot across the bridge of the nose between the eyes, and I tell you he came near losing the sight of both eyes from it. The same shot killed Hollis, Cosby was shot in two by a shell; all of this in the thicket above mentioned." 3

"On the day of the battle, December 31, 1862, the Brigade made two advances; the first time they were repulsed and driven back, but on the next advance the line was so perfect it looked more like a dress parade than their line of battle, and it carried everything before it that time, in their charge upon the Federal battery about five or six hundred yards distant and through a field to a Cedar glade to where the battery was stationed. You can be assured they did effective work when I say in a Plumb orchard of half an acre in extent just in front of the Federal battery you could almost traverse the whole field on the bodies of the dead and wounded Yankees." 3

"Here the regiment lost Lieutenant-colonel Autry, who had so lately come to us, and many of its best company officers and quite heavily of the rank and file. As soon as it was known that Lieutenant-colonel was dead the regiment almost to a man petitioned Gen. Bragg to again send us Col. Hays, who remained in command until in the spring, when field officers were chosen from the company officers of the regiment." 3

"We were in the whole fight at Murfreesboro during the week, and in the retrograde movement with the army back to Shelbyville, and where the army finally went into winter quarters late in January 1863. About this time we lose sight of our first Colonel Jones, for some cause I cannot now recall, and I never heard of him again." 3

During the battle of Murfreesboro, Gen. Patton Anderson was in command of Walthall's Brigade, which was stationed in the line of battle, December 28, the left extending into a dense Cedar forest, the right next to Chalmer's Brigade. The Twenty-ninth, on the right, was the only regiment in an open field, and the men made rifle pits for protection. There was skirmishing with the Federal line, posted along the round the forest and cane break, during the next to days. On the morning of the 31st, the brigade attacked, the Twenty-seventh being the last, according to the plan of battle, along the whole line to advance. They were immediate swept by a heavy fire of artillery from the front, and partly enfilading the line. Anderson reported: "The ordeal to which they were subjected was a severe one, but the task was undertaken with that spirit and courage which always deserves success and seldom fails achieving it. As often as their ranks were shattered and broken by grape and canister did they rally, reform and renewed the attack under the leadership of their gallant officers. They were ordered to take the battery at all hazards and they obeyed the order, not however, without heavy loses of officers and men. Not Far from were the batteries were playing, and while cheering and encouraging his men forward, Lieut.-Col. James L. Autry, commanding the Twenty-seventh Mississippi, fell, pierced through the head by a Minnie ball." There was some confusion in the regiment until they were reformed by he senior Captain, E.R. Neilson, who was seriously wounded afterwards in another part of the field. Colonel Jones had gone to the rear for medical attention. Finally the batteries were taken. One company entirely, of sharpshooters, posted in a log house near the battery, taken by the Twenty-seventh, Twenty-ninth and Thirtieth, was captured by the Twenty-seventh. The casualties of the Twenty-seventh were 11 killed, 71 wounded, 2 missing. 3

On January 2nd, the brigade, which had been assigned to the position on the river front held by Chalmers' Brigade, was ordered across the river to support General Breckenridge, was recalled, and later in the afternoon was sent again. Of this movement General Bragg, wrote in his report that on hearing of the defeat of Breckenridge: "Anderson's fine brigade of Mississippians, the nearest body of troops, was promptly ordered to his relief. On reaching the field and moving forward, Anderson found himself in front of Breckenridge's infantry and soon encountered the enemy's light troops close under our artillery, which had been left without support. This noble brigade, under its cool and gallant chief, drove the enemy back and saved all our guns not captured before its arrival." Breckenridge reformed his line after dark to the left and rear of the Walthall Brigade. 4

According to official records, the 27th Mississippi regiment suffered 83 causalities total during the Murfreesboro battle. 1

ORDER OF BATTLE CONFEDERATE FORCES
MIDDLE TENNESSEE CAMPAIGN - BATTLE OF MURFREESBORO
DECEMBER 31, 1862- JANUARY 3, 1863
ARMY OF TENNESSEE - C.S.A.
Commanding: General Braxton Bragg
34,739 Men
POLK'S CORPS:
Commanding: Lt.Gen. Leonidas Polk

FIRST DIVISION:			
Commanding: Maj.Gen. Benjamin F. Cheatham			
	1st BRIGADE:		
	Commanding: Brig.Gen. Daniel S. Donelson		
		(5 Tennessee Regts)	
	2nd BRIGADE:		
	Commanding: Brig.Gen. Alexander P. Stewart		
		(6 Tennessee Regts)	
	3rd BRIGADE:		
	Commanding: Brig.Gen. George Maney		
		(5 Tennessee Regts)	
	4th BRIGADE: (Smith)		
	Commanding: Col. Vaughan Jr.		
		(5 Tennessee Regts, 1 Texas Regt)	
SECOND DIVISION:			
Commanding: Maj.Gen. Jones Withers			
	1st BRIGADE:		
	Commanding: Col. Loomis		
		(5 Alabama Regts, 1 Louisiana Regt)	
	2nd BRIGADE:		
	Commanding: Brig.Gen. Chalmers		
		(4 Mississippi Regts)	
	3rd BRIGADE:		
	Commanding: Brig.Gen. Anderson		
		45th Alabama	
		24th Mississippi	
		27th Mississippi	
		29th Mississippi	

			30th Mississippi
			39th North Carolina
			Mo Btry
		4th BRIGADE:	
		Commanding: Col. Manigault	
			(2 Alabama Regts, 2 S.C. Regts)
HARDEE'S CORPS:			
Commanding: Lt.Gen. William Hardee			
	FIRST DIVISION:		
	Commanding: Maj.Gen. John C. Breckinridge		
		1st BRIDAGE:	
		Commanding: Col.Adams	
			(4 Louisiana Regts, 1 Alabama Regt)
		2nd BRIGADE:	
		Commanding: Col. Palmer	
			(5 Tennessee Regts)
		3th BRIGADE:	
		Commanding: Brig.Gen. Preston	
			(3 Florida Regts, 1 Tenn Regt, 1 N.C. Regt)
		4th BRIGADE:	
		Commanding: Brig.Gen. Hanson	
			(4 Kentucky Regts, 1 Alabama Regt)
		JACKSON'S BRIGADE:	
		Commanding: Brig.Gen. Jackson	
			(2 Mississippi Regts, 1 Georgia Regt)
	SECOND DIVISION:		
	Commanding: Maj.Gen. Patrick Celburne		
		2nd BRIGADE:	
		Commanding: Brig.Gen. Saint John Liddell	
			(5 Arkansas Regts)
		1st BRIGADE:	
		Commanding: Brig.Gen.L. E. Polk	
			(3 Ark Regts, 2 Tenn Regts, 1 CSA Regt)
		3rd BRIGADE:	
		Commanding: Brig.Gen. Bushrod Johnson	
			(5 Tennessee Regts, 1 CSA Regt)
		4th BRIGADE:	
		Commanding: Brig.Gen. Sterling Wood	

			(2 Alabama Regst, 1 Miss Regt, 1 CSA Regt)
	MC CROWN'S DIVISION:		
	Commanding: Mj.Gen. J.P. Mc Crown		
		1st BRIGADE:	
		Commanding: Brig.Gen. Ector	
		(4 Texas Cav (Foot) Regts)	
		2nd BRIGADE:	
		Commanding: Brig.Gen.Rains	
			(2 Georgia Regts, 1 Tenn Regt, 1 N.C. Regt)
		3rd BRIGADE:	
		Commanding: Brig.Gen. McNair	
			(4 Arkansas Regts)
	CAVALRY DIVISION:		
	Commanding: Brig.Gen. Joseph Wheeler		
		Wheeler's BRIGADE:	
			(3 Alabama Regts, 1 Tenn Regt, 1 CSA Regt)
		Wharton's BRIGADE:	
		Commanding: Brig.Gen. Wharton	
			(3 Tenn Regts, 2 Ga Regts, 2 CSA Regts, 1 Tx & Ala)
		Bufor's BRIGADE:	
		Commanding: Brig.Gen. Buford	
			(3 Kentucky Regts)
		Pegram's BRIGADE:	
		Commanding: Col. Pegram	
			(1 Ga Regt, 1 Louisiana Regt)
		DIVISION ARTY: (3 Btrys)	
Re: Bush, Bryan S., The Civil War Battles of the Western Theater; 1998; Pgs 44; 45-48.			

MURFREESBORO, TENNESSEE 1862-63

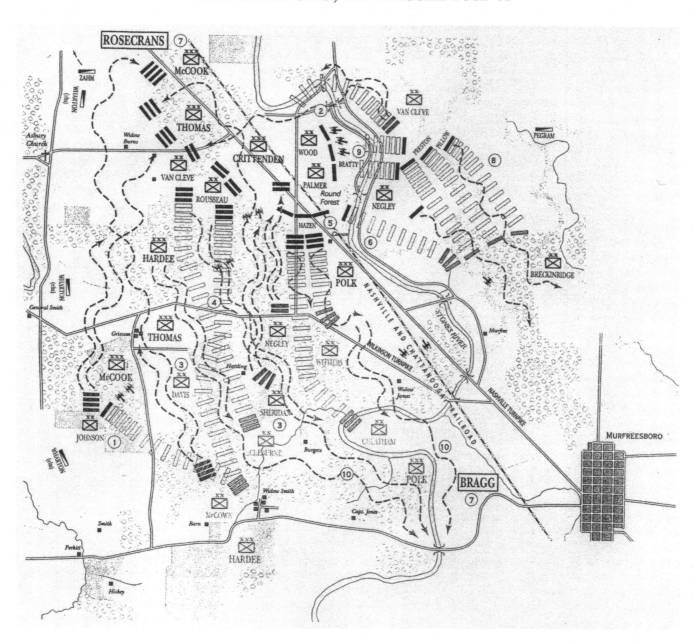

RE: THE CIVIL WAR OF THE WESTERN THEATER

M

The Mission for Tullahoma . . .

CHAPTER V.

TULLAHOMA, TENNESSEE: JUNE 1863.

Sgt. Jarman continues, "After the army fell back from Murfreesboro and was established in winter quarters, near Shelbyville, the field and staff of the 27th Mississippi regiment was re-organized by making Capt. Campbell, of Company E, Colonel; Capt. Jones of Company C, Lieutenant-colonel, and Capt. McLemore of Company B, Major. Lieutenant W.H. Saunders, of Company K, became our Captain. Lieutenant A.V. Snowden, First Lieutenant, Mr. W.A. McMillan, Second Lieutenant. During the winter Mr. McMillan had been detailed and sent home after clothing for the company that had the previous spring been shipped back home to Aberdeen, and I can assure you the writer and whole company enjoyed getting their overcoats and good under clothing after the exposure around Murfreesboro." 3

"On the march from Murfreesboro it was amusing to see the different men in the Company gathering sage out of gardens along the road, so they could enjoy the luxury of a cup of sage tea at night. Just imagine to yourself a whole company drinking sage tea at once, what grand enjoyment!" 3

"While encamped at or near Shelbyville I do not recollect what we did, except drill, unless it was to guard some of the many still houses near there to keep the men from getting as we then called it, 'pine top whisky,' but since then it has been given the name of Mountain Dew." 3

"While the army was near Shelbyville, and I was at home on sick furlough, the brigade was sent to Lewisburg, Tennessee, about 20 miles from the main army to do outpost picket duty, but some of the men claimed when I got back it was only to furlough the whole of Walthall's brigade and given them a chance to get butter milk. You can imagine that they had a good time when I say after a lapse 27 years some who are now grandfathers laugh heartily at how the brigade and regimental staff officers and all others who the fair ladies of Lewisburg and surrounding country. The command also had nearly every day chicken fighting for be it known that there was plenty of game chickens around Lewisburg at first, but deponent saith not how many were there when the command left to again rejoin the army at Shelbyville." 3

"I rejoined my company there, in June 1863 time enough to be on the retreat from Middle Tennessee. I was detailed with others during that trip and sent to Decatur on the Nashville & Chattanooga railroad, to do guard duty, and while there I first remember seeing Gen. N.B. Forrest. We remained here until the last train was leaving, when we turned over our position to cavalry and started to rejoin our command at the foot of Cumberland Mountains, and helped that night and part of the next day to push up the wagon train that was crossing the mountains with us. While on this trip we enjoyed the green apples of the country nearly as well as did the ripe apples of the winter before. Rations ran short on this trip with us, and when flour was issued to us we made it up on our oil cloths, and some baked it on flat rocks, and some rolled it around their ram-rode and baked that way, for our wagons with cooking utensils was not near us." 3

"Before we arrived at the Tennessee River there was a detail sent that brought back to us cooked provisions for one day. We crossed the river above Bridgeport, Ala., and below Chattanooga, on a pontoon bridge, then we traveled near the railroad but on the dirt road from there to Chattanooga, when we got there we were a muddy, dirty set, for it had rained on us for nearly a week, and we had to wade all the branches and creeks as we came to them; and fortunately for myself, I was nearly the only man in the Company that night put on an entire clean suit of clothes. I was just from home and had in addition to my suit for my brother, but he had gone home on wounded furlough and I had a double supply. Nearly the first thing that greeted us after we got in camp at Chattanooga was a veritable peanut stand. Some men in the Company had managed through the teamsters of wagon train to get a couple of sacks of goober peas for sale; and as the command had had nothing of the kind for several days, it took one man nearly all his time to serve them out and make the necessary change, and the whole lot was soon sold, but next day and during the time we were there the goober peas were plentiful in camp. Next day, as soon as the men had time to forage around, it was discovered that there was a market garden near us with some three acres or more of long stem blue collards; but they were greens, and the brigade was "hankering" for something of that kind, and it was not very long until we dug up the entire patch; for be it not said that a soldier would eat almost anything in season or out of season. We remained here some 10 days or two weeks, when our brigade was again sent on special detached service from Chattanooga, Tennessee, to Atlanta, Georgia." 3

The Battle of Chickamauga . . .

CHAPTER VI.

CHICKAMUAGA, GEORGIA: SEPTEMBER 1863

Sgt. Jarman continues: "When the brigade left Chattanooga for Atlanta, Georgia, in July 1863 rumor said it was on account of an expected raid from the Federal cavalry on Atlanta, our base of supplies, and the arsenal situated there. We arrived there in the midst of the peach and watermelon season, and the country tributary to Atlanta raises fine peaches, at least it did when we were there in 1863. The different regiments were stationed at various places around the city, and one left to guard the railroad bridge across the Chattahoochee River. Soon after arriving in Atlanta, the command was paid off, so the men could spend their money, and they did enjoy investing it in peaches, melons, Pinetop whiskey and many other luxuries that for sometime had been unknown to the soldiers of our command. We had everyday old fashioned peach pies baked in an oven, then we would go to the houses close to camp and engage dinner at times for a whole mess at once, which was generally vegetables, fried chicken or chicken pie, but always ended in peach pie. Then when we got a chance to go to town (which was quite often), we could get peaches and honey, and we all know its merits too well to discuss them here." 3

"But lo and behold, the day came when it was shown what our real business was there. The bugle sounded and the drums beat the long roll, and we fell in line and marched in a double quick to our positions, leaving only those on duty as camp guard who were on post. A strong picket line was formed around the whole place, when enough men were sent back to make a full camp guard, to care for camp and cook for the pickets. Then orders were issued to let everybody come in, but no one to pass out without a special permit. Then the horses and mules began to come in from the surrounding country for the balance of the day and all night, their owners expecting any minute the Federal cavalry to get their stock unless they were brought to Atlanta for protection. Next morning there were details sent out and we began to gather in and turn over to the post quartermaster all the stock found in Atlanta, that the best and most suitable might be retained for recruiting the artillery and cavalry horses, and mules for the supply train of the Army of Tennessee, for the coming fall campaign. I tell you we got fine carriage horses out of parlors, from sitting rooms, and in one instance from up stairs. One fine spau of horses we thought had some got away, but after the day, when the pickets were relieved, we found them, accidentally, in a hazelnut thicket in 300 yards of camp. We remained here now only a few days longer, as we had accomplished the purpose we were sent to Atlanta for—the impressments of horses for the army. We left Atlanta for Chickamauga Station and were assigned to Liddell's Division, Walker's reserve corps. While at Atlanta my father sent me another servant by the name of Rafe, who at different times hereafter will come up. He has been in Aberdeen for some years as a common loafer, and calls himself, Raford Hooks. Pity a good negro should become so worthless." 3

"When we got to Chickamauga Station and were put in the reserve corps we thought that we would have a good time but we learned that in the army parlance reserve did not mean reserve at all, but it meant the first in and the last out when it came to a battle." 3

"While here during the last days of August and the first of September, we enjoyed roasting ears of corn and field beans (not peas). While here, one Sunday morning, Tom Townsend, (the poor fellow had to a certain extent lost his reason, particularly whenever he saw a man stroke his beard or twist his mustache) walked up to Lieutenant McMillan, who was stroking his beard, and ask him why he thus insulted him. Lieutenant McMillan assured him that he meant no insult but to no avail, he had to be sent to the tent until after inspection, when his delusion had left him. He was killed soon after at the battle of Chickamauga; his one fault was his imagining himself insulted; he was a good soldier, but partly demented after the death of his brother, J.B. Townsend, at Murfreesboro." 3

"We spent several days before the battle of Chickamauga in chasing after scouting parties of the enemy in the caves and hollows of the mountains, and one day when rations were particularly scarce with us, I had Rafe off at a house near by cooking a chicken pie for the mess, and Jesse Carroll, of the mess, had in his haversack some crackers and bacon that he had brought with him from Atlanta, but when ask to divide, denied having anything. Jesse was put on a water detail and sent about a half mile for water, and in an unlucky moment gave me his haversack to keep until he returned, and while he was gone I called the mess together and we ate everything he had, and when he got back be could truthfully say he had nothing to eat. He reared and cussed, and to me his favorite expressions said "I wish to G__ we would have peaches before day, and that he had died before he was born," but that evening when Rafe came up with a big bucket of chicken pie and roasted potatoes, Jesse got in a better humor, and ate a hearty dinner with us, and began again to accumulate eating for us; but after that he always divided, but would grumble." 3

"Finally, on Friday evening, September 18th, 1863, we struck the enemy on a left wheel of the brigade, and when the regiments on the right of the brigade struck Chickamauga River, the enemy had crossed the bridge and escaped, but we exchanged shots with them at long range. The enemy having the bridge covered with artillery, we faced to the right and went along the river and wade over and forced them to leave he bridge by a flank movement. That night the corps lay on their arms in double lines, one on each side of the road. Next, morning while still lying there waiting for rations and water. Longstreet's Corps from Virginia, passed with high glee, and said they had come to show us how they fought in Virginia. They came for wool but were nearly shorn when they got back that night, for they caught a Tartar that day. As soon as Longstreet passed us we were called to attention and every man told to examine his gun and see that it was all right. We then marched back on some road we came the evening before a short distance, and again Company K was put on the skirmish line and the order to forward given. We could hear firing, but thought it was cavalry three or four miles off, but we had not gone over half a mile until we found the cavalry horses and holders, and by the time we got thro' the horses stray balls began to fall. Soon we had the order, skirmishers double quick, through an open woods with only low post oak bushes about waist high, our objective point being a battery of eight guns in front of us. In our excitement and charge we ran through part of the line of Federal infantry in front of the guns, and I thought our time then had about come, but they surrendered to us and we pushed on to the battery that was just beginning to fire grape and canister on the bridge that was not more than 75 yards behind us; but J.S. Thompson, Bill Woodford, Green Westbrook and myself, I think between us, killed the last gunner at the battery, when each of us bounced astride of a gun and yelled our loudest, then we turned the loaded guns on the Yankees and gave their own grape. We could not then get the guns off the field, for all the horses were killed. All of our regiment had been well drilled in artillery, and at that time it came into good use. Every regiment capturing artillery in battle was entitled to the crossed cannon and name of battle on their regimental flag, and that was a grand inducement to get men to charge batteries where it looked like instant death. In a short while the enemy rallied and retook the battery from us, and then we again took it from them and finally got the most of it off the field. Near this battery that evening word was passed up our line as were lying down that there was a Yankee sharpshooter in a certain fence, killing a man every time he shot, and if somebody didn't kill him the line would have to be moved. I volunteered to try and get him, and went some forty steps in front of the skirmish line, where there were some logs lying, asking the balance of my file of four to watch close for me. At first I could not see the man but could see the smoke of his gun, but he soon exposed himself to ram his gun, that was my chance and I fired at him about 125 yards, striking him under the left shoulder blade. He lay in the same place until the next Tuesday, when I was over the battlefield again. I then did not go entirely back to the skirmish line, but only part of the way and sat down by a large tree with my back to it expecting the line to advance. I jumped up and looked around and a Yankee and a real live one at that, dodged behind a tree about 80 yards off, then we passed several shots, then I called upon my file to come to my assistance, and nobly did they respond, and for his audacity when we went off the field he carried a Minnie ball through his leg, turning summersaults like a chicken with his head off." 3

"Our line remained in the same position until after sundown, when Cleburne' Division relieved us and passed over us, pushed forward their line and drove the enemy about a half mile, where they bivouacked, we bivouacked closed by when we were relieved." 3

"During this day's engagement, I do not now remember all the killed and wounded; T.B. Townsend was killed for one, and H.D. Spratt was wounded, the shot entering at the knee and was cut out near the hip, and eventually caused his death. Early next morning Rafe was on hand again with something for the mess to eat, but it was mostly roasted potatoes, but they filled the empty stomachs. It seemed Gen. Bragg's idea that hungry men fought the best because they were mad, but after each battle he always feed well. About 10 O'clock Sunday morning, September 20th, 1863 we moved from the position we had held the night before occupied, towards the right of our line, and where the cavalry were to support us. Nothing worth mentioning occurred until towards middle of the evening, when Company K was again deployed as skirmishers and the line advanced across the road leading to Chattanooga, where we were as hotly pressed as at any time during the battle." 3

"The enemy struck our line on the left flank and engaged only one regiment or part of regiment at a time, and from our position on the skirmish line, nearly three hundred yards in front, we could see the brigade beaten back a regiment at a time. We held our position until the regiment broke to the colors, when we began a race which is only equaled by horses on some famous race course, we were so hotly pursued. When we crossed the road all pursuit seemed to stop, for the Yankees were fighting for a road to escape on. Here it was Gen. Walthall was rallying his men (and here it was that the root was cut that was presented to Gen. Walthall, so full of shot from the battlefield of Chickamauga, at the reunion in Aberdeen last fall). I at once, from the description, remembered the place in a small hollow or branch, where he rallied the command, and time enough to recapture some of our company that was captured on that never to be forgotten race. At this place our muster roll shows that Lt. W.A. McMillan, J.M. Fears, R.H. Peters, Wilson Whatley and John Whatley were captured. Here it was that Gen. Forrest, in attempting to shell over our line and shell the enemy, was in fact with his howitzers shelling our line from behind while the enemy shelled us in front; and after we had made the celebrated race above spoken of, to where Gen. Walthall, rallying the command, cursed us and said that as Mississippians we had disgraced the cradles in which we were rocked, and demanded we at once advance on the enemy, and which advance resulted in our recapturing part of the company." 3

"On this race I saw Lieutenant Reid, of the 24th Mississippi, dropped his sword accidentally and he ran back, regained the sword and came out all right. We lay on our arms all night near here, and next morning we had a full supply of rations issued to us, when J.W. Peck and myself were part of a scouting detail sent out to see how many prisoners and what else we could find. We returned to the command about 12 O'clock with some twenty prisoners, and we were also detailed to take them back to the Provost Marshal of the army at the Big Spring, across Chickamauga River, so we that evening and next morning passed over all the ground on which our brigade had fought. On arriving at the Provost Marshal's that night we were put as guard around the prisoners that had been captured during the whole battle. Next morning the Provost Marshal wanted us to go as guard with prisoner's to Andersonville, and proffered to send a courier to the brigade to account for us and get a description list of us, but Mr. Peck wanted to hear from his wife, and would not consent, as he had been for a time detailed as non-commissioned officer and put in charge of the detail. We would have had a good time as our servants were with us and had clothes for us. So we were given a special pass to cross the battlefield to keep from being arrested as stragglers, and late that evening we rejoined our command going towards Chattanooga. (The reason there is so much of myself in this, is the impossibility for one man to see all that occurred on a skirmish line from 75 to 150 yards long when he had so much to attract his attention in his immediate front!)" 3

During this time the Twenty-seventh Mississippi regiment was assigned to Walthall's' Brigade, Hindmen's' Division, First Corps, Army of Tennessee, and remained until November 1863. 2

The official casualty reports for the 27th Mississippi, from the battle of Chickamauga, September 19-20, 1863 reflected the loss of 117 men. 1

Another Official description of the battle, "In Chickamauga campaign Walthall's Brigade and Gavan's Arkansas Brigade constituted Liddell's Division of W.H.T. Walker's Corps. Walthall's Brigade, on September 18, forced a Federal command from Alexander's bridge, but finding the bridge destroyed were compelled to cross at Bryam's Ford, after which, on the next day, the marched to the north and went into battle in that confused area where Ector and Wilson had been worsted. The Twenty-seventh, under Col. James A. Campbell, participated in the charge that ran over King's Brigade of United States regulars as they were changing front, capturing 400 prisoners and a battery. This was in the woods, between fortified position that Thomas held next day, and the creek. Being flanked and losing many officers and men, the Twenty-seventh and other regiments fell back in some confusion. The next morning they moved a mile to the left and then three miles to the north, and went into battle on the Chattanooga road, which they occupied and crossed in the rear of Gen. Thomas. Here most of the skirmishers of the brigade were captured, and Lieut.-Col. Jones, then acting as field officer of the day, was wounded. At this time only three were left on the field of ten officers of the brigade. Colonel Campbell commended the conduct of Captains Kennedy, Company G; Baugh of Company F, and Boyd of Company E. Casualties of the regiment, 10 killed, 88 wounded, 19 missing. 4

ORDER OF BATTLE CONFEDERATE FORCES			
NORTHERN GEORGIA CAMPAIGN - BATTLE OF CHICKAMAUGA			
SEPTEMBER 19-20, 1863			
ARMY OF TENNESSEE - C.S.A.			
Commanding: General Braxton Bragg			
66,300 Men			
POLK'S(I) CORPS: RIGHT WING/			
Commanding: Lt.Gen. Leonidas Polk			
	FIRST (Cheatham's) DIVISION:		
	Commanding: Maj.Gen. Benjamin F. Cheatham		
		JACKSON'S BRIGADE:	
			(2 Mississippi Regts, 1 Ga Regt, 2 Tenn Regts)
		3rd (Maney) BRIGADE:	
			(5 Tennessee Regts)
		4th (Smith's/Vaughan's) BRIGADE:	
			(5 Tennessee Regts)
		1st (Donelson's/Wright's) BRIGADE:	
			(6 Tennessee Regts)
		(Stewart's/Strahl's) BRIGADE:	
			(6 Tennessee Regts)
		Cheathan's DIVISION ARTY: (5 Btrys)	
		Commanding: Maj. Smith	
(Hardee's/Hill's) (II) CORPS:			
Commanding: Lt.Gen Daniel H. Hill			
	SECOND (Cleburne's) DIVISION:		
	Commanding: Maj.Gen. Patrick Cleburne		
		4th (Wood's) BRIGADE:	
			(4 Alabama Regts)
		POLK'S BRIGADE:	
			(3 Tenn Regts, 2 CSA Regts, 1 Ark Regt)
		DESHLER'S BRIGADE:	
			(7 Texas Regts, 2 Arkansas Regts)
		Cleburn's DIVISION ARTY: (3 Btrys)	
		Commanding: Capt. Henry Semple	

FIRST (Breckenridge's) DIVISION:		
Commanding: Maj.Gen. John C. Breckinridge		
	1st (Adams') BRIDAGE:	
		(5 Louisiana Regts, 1 Alabama Regt)
	3th (Preston's/Stovall's) BRIGADE:	
		(3 Florida Regts, 1 Ga Regt, 1 N.C. Regt)
	4th (Hanson/Helm's) BRIGADE:	
		(4 Kentucky Regts, 1 Alabama Regt)
	Breckinridge's DIVISION ARTY: (4 Btrys)	
	Commandin: Maj. Rice Graves	
WALKER"S RESERVE CORPS:		
Commanding: Maj.Gen. W. H. T. Walker		
	WALKER'S DIVISION:	
	Commanding: Brig.Gen. States Rights Gist	
	GIST'S BRIGADE:	
		(2 S.C. Regts, 1 Ga Regt)
	ECTOR'S BRIGADE:	
		(3 Texas Regts, 1 N.C. Regt)
	WILSON'S BRIGADE:	
		(3 Georgia Regts, 1 Louisiana Regt)
	Walker's DIVISION ARTY: (2 Btrys)	
	Commanding: Unknown	
	LIDDELL'S DIVISION:	
	Commanding: Brig.Gen. St. John R. Liddell	
	2nd (Liddell's/Govan's) BRIGADE:	
		(7 Arkansas Regts, 1 Louisiana Regt)
	3rd (Anderson's/Walthall's) BRIGADE:	
	Commanding: Brig.Gen. Edward C. Walthall	
		24th Mississippi
		27th Mississippi
		29th Mississippi
		30th Mississippi
		34th Mississippi
	Liddell's DIVISION ARTY: (2 Btrys)	
	Commanding: Capt. C. Scott	
LONGSTREET'S CORPS: LEFT WING		

Commanding: Lt.Gen. James Longstreet			
BUCKNER'S CORPS:			
Commanding: Maj.Gen. Simon Buckner			
	STEWART'S DIVISION:		
	Commanding: Maj.Gen. Alexander P. Stewart		
		BATE'S BRIGADE:	
			(3 Tennessee Regts, 1 Ala Regt, 1 Ga Regt)
		CLAYTON'S BRIGADE:	
			(3 Alabama Regts)
		2nd (Palmer's/Brown's) BRIGADE:	
			(4 Tennessee Regts)
		3rd (Johnson's) BRIGADE:	
			(4 Tennessee Regts, 1 CSA Regt)
		Stewart's DIVISION ARTY: (3 Btrys)	
		Commanding: Maj. J.W. Eldridge	
		(York's) Co E/9th Ga Arty Bn	
	Preston's DIVISION:		
	Commanding: Brig.Gen. William Preston		
		GRACIE'S BRIGADE:	
			(1 Tenn Regt, 1 Ala Regt, 1 Hillards Legion)
		KELLY'S BRIGADE:	
			(1 Ky Regt, 1 N.C. Regt, 1 Ga Regt, 1 Va Regt)
		TRIGG'S BRIGADE:	
			(3 Florida Regts, 1 Va Regt)
		RESERVE CORPS ARTY: (4 Btrys)	
		Commanding: Maj. S. Williams	
	SECOND (Wither's/Hindman's) DIVISION:		
	Commanding: Maj.Gen. Thomas C. Hindman		
		1st (Loomis/Deas') BRIGADE:	
			(5 Alabama Regts)
		2nd (Chalmer'sAnderson's) BRIGADE:	
			(5 Mississippi Regts)
		4th (Manigualt's) BRIGADE:	
			(3 Alabama Regts, 2 S.C. Regts)
	Johnson's DIVISION:		

Commmanding: Brig.Gen. Bushrod Johnson				
		GREGG'S BRIGADE:		
			(5 Tennessee Regts, 1 Texas Regt)	
		MC NAIR'S BRIGADE:		
			(5 Arkansas Regts, 1 N.C. Regt)	

LONGSTREET"S CORPS:

Commanding: Lt.Gen. James Longstreet

		KERSHAW'S BRIGADE:		
			(5 South Carolina Regts)	
		HUMPHREY'S BRIGADE:		
			(4 Mississippi Regts)	
	HOOD'S DIVISION:			
	Commanding: MajGen. Jobn B. Hood			
		LAW'S BRIGADE:		
			(5 Alabama Regts)	
		ROBERTSON'S BRIGADE:		
			(3 Texas Regts, 1 Arkansas Regt)	
		BENNING'S BRIGADE:		
			(4 Georgia Regts)	
		RESERVE DIVISION ARTY: (5 Btrys)		
		Commanding: Maj. Felix Robertson		

WHEELER'S CAV CORPS:

Commanding: Maj.Gen. Joseph Wheeler

	WHARTON'S CAV DIVISION:			
	Commanding: Brig.Gen. John Wharton			
		1st CAV BRIGADE:		
			(3 Georgia Regts, 1 Alabama Regt)	
		2nd CAV BRIGADE:		
			(2 Tex Regts, 1 Ky Regt, 1 Tenn Regt, 1 CSA Regt)	
	MARTIN'S CAV DIVISION:			
	Commanding: Brig.Gen. William Martin			
		1st CAV BRIGADE:		
			(3 Alabama Regts, 1 CSA Regt)	
		2nd CAV BRIGADE:		

FORREST'S CAV CORPS:			
Commanding: Brig.Gen. Nathan B. Forrest			
	ARMSTRONG'S CAV DIVISION:		
	Commanding: Brig.Gen. Frank Armstrong		
		ARMSTRONG'S BRIGADE:	
			(1 Ky Regt, 1 Tenn Regt, 1 Ala Regt)
		FORREST CAV BRIGADE:	
			(5 Tennesse Regts)
	PEGRAM'S CAV DIVISION:		
	Commanding: Brig.Gen. John Pegram		
		DAVIDSON'S CAV BRIGADE:	
			(2 Ga Regts, 1 N.C. Regt, 1 CSA Regt, 1 Ruckers Legion)
		SCOTT'S CAV BRIGADE:	
			(2 Tenn Regts, 1 La Regt, 1 Ky Regt)
Re: Tucker, Glenn; Chickamauga; Morningside Press, 1976.			
Bush, Bryan S.; The Civil War Battles of the Western Theater; 1998; Pgs 59-61			

WALKER COUNTY, GEORGIA 1863

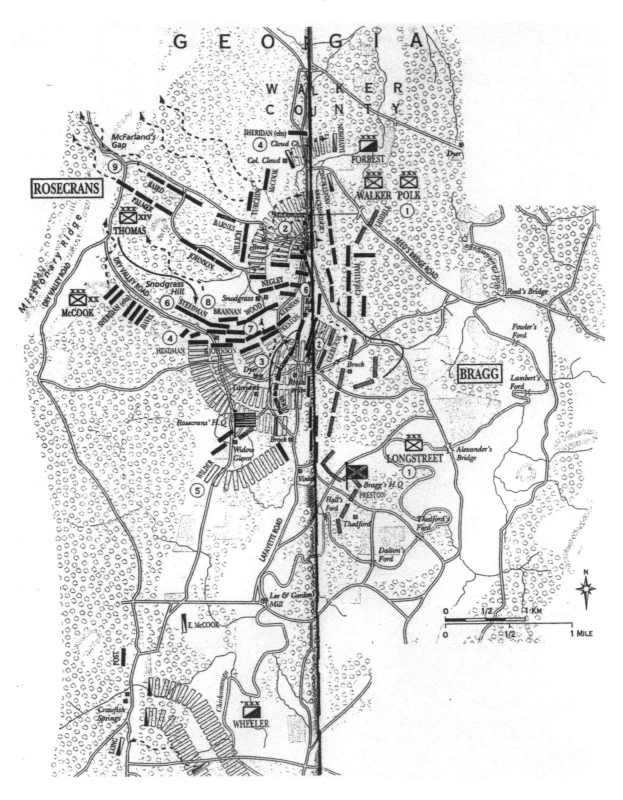

RE: THE CIVIL WAR OF THE WESTERN THEATER
M

CHATTANOOGA SIEGE, TENNESSEE: SEPTEMBER 1863

The Jarman journal states "After we arrived in front of Chattanooga, it was several days before our lines were established in the position that we occupied until the last of November. Our picket line was some distance in front of the line of battle, which was at first formed on top of Missionary Ridge. While establishing our picket line one night we drove in the Federal pickets so far that we could see the gleaming and flashing of their guns, both muskets and cannon, on the forts around Chattanooga. That night, I think, we finally established our pickets in the position held afterwards. We could hear the long roll beaten, and the Federal wagon train hurrying across the Tennessee River on the pontoon bridges all night, for they momentarily expected to be attacked by the whole army, and wanted to have their train where it would be secure. At the time it was thought if we had pushed on the night we could have easily taken the place, for the army was flushed with victory and the Federals oppressed with defeat." 3

"Just after the picket line was established that night the skirmish line was withdrawn and we fell back to the picket line. After this, there were no more demonstrations while we stayed in front of Chattanooga, at least on our part of the line that I remember. By mutual understanding between the two armies we ceased to fire at each other on the picket line and this made picket duty much safer with us, for we were in no danger of being shot on the sly either day or night. I now think the agreement was brought about by flag of truce for the exchange of some prisoners still in the hands of each army." 3

"We continued to do guard duty for the month of October, or at least the greater part, when our command was moved back a short distance and the men fixed up more comfortably for a few days, when it was said we would go into winter quarters. While here I received my overcoat and some other things from home, and some money, by the courtesy of a Mr. Drake who had to refugee from Tennessee and had gone to the army to visit his son in a Tennessee regiment." 3

"We did not, however, remain in this position very long, but our brigade was sent to the front of Lookout Mountain to relieve part of Longstreet's Corps that was ordered to Knoxville; and here it was on Lookout Mountain that rations became very scare during our ten day stay there in November. One day our issue rations consisted of three crackers and about two tablespoons of sugar, but thanks to Rafe, who was with the wagon train, we, that is my mess, kept a full supply of bacon on hand for each day. While here on Lookout Mountain we did picket at the foot of the mountain, on a creek, we called Lookout creek, and near the railroad. While here the two picket lines at many places were not more than forty yards apart. We could see and here them relieving their pickets, and they could see us. Each party kept a fire at the vidette post, day and night. We even met halfway in the creek, where it was shallow and on the shoals to swap newspapers, canteens, tobacco for coffee, and I have seen some swap hats and shoes, and talk for half an hour at a time, but this was only when no officer was present on either side." 3

The Defense of, and the Battling for Lookout Mountain and Missionary Ridge—Chattanooga . . .

CHAPTER VII.

CHATTANOOGA, TENNESSEE: 23 NOVEMBER 1863

"Well, all good times have to come to end, and easy picket duty shared that fate, for on November 24th, 1863, we were attacked on Lookout mountain, it was said, by Gen. Grant and his entire army that had just arrived to join Gen. Thomas, from Vicksburg, and the way they swarmed and crowded up Lookout mountain that morning against only one brigade of Confederates, was a sight to see. We were simply crushed by numbers, and it was the tallest fighting I was ever in, for during the fight it was cloudy and a dense cloud settled down over us so we could not distinguish friend from foe over twenty steps. Some of the men that escaped scaled the face of the mountain and some escaped by way of a white house on the side of the mountain, called the Craven house. I came out by the house, and jumped over two cliffs, nearly twenty feet high. Here Lieutenant A.V. Snowden of Company K was killed, and the following made prisoners: Sergeants J.W. Marshall and T.D. Williamson; Privates: Jas. H. Cheek, B.F. Gibson, R.E. Hill, W.M. Nash, James M. Smith and James Thrailkil." 3

"We finally left Lookout Mountain during the night and camped in the valley between the mountain and Missionary Ridge. During the day it was said the brigade lost more that nine hundred men killed and captured on Lookout Mountain, and among the captured was Col. Campbell of our regiment. Next day, November 25th, 1863 we joined the main army on Missionary Ridge, but we looked more like a regiment than a brigade, and a small regiment at that. Here we participated in the battle of Missionary Ridge; and during the day I witnessed one of the greatest sights I ever saw, from a high point on the ridge near the centre of the Confederate line. By stretching out my arms from my body and looking from point of hand to point of hand, I could see the combined armies both Confederate and Federal under arms and fighting. I suppose in all nearly 80,000 men, for it was estimated, I think, that Gen. Bragg had with him some 30,000 men. We did not do much fighting that day until late in evening, near sundown, when the lines were broken to our left and Gen. Cheatham ordered Gen. Walthall to form his command at the right angle to the ridge, or across it, and hold it at all hazards." 3

"We quickly formed, and Gen. Walthall in front on his horse telling the men to keep quiet and not be excited (when he was wounded in the foot, but never left the command until we were safe back two or three days afterwards). We made a small charge which checked the enemy for the time and held them in check until after night, when we quickly withdrew our lines, and the army began retreat from Missionary Ridge. That night a detail was sent ahead to Chickamauga Station to draw rations for the different companies. Tom Farr was the detail for Companies F and K, (we were now consolidated with Company F, but each company kept its own organization) after he had drawn for

"CAUSE FOR THANKSGIVING." BY GILBERT GAUL, HARPER'S WEEKLY, 1867

Civil War: Battle of Lookout Mountain, 1863

"BATTLE OF LOOKOUT MOUNTAIN" BY KURZ & ALLISON / LIBRARY OF CONGRESS

Nov. 20-23—*Battle of N*

us he let somebody steal the whole three days' rations. When we came up and found what had been done, Capt. Baugh, Company F, ask for a volunteer detail from the companies of six men to go to the station and draw or steal more, and they drew more for companies F and K than all the balance of the regiment had to together. We had so much next morning that the commander of Company L complained to the Colonel commanding of the regiment, Lieut.-Col. Jones, stating that Companies F and K had his men's rations, but Capt. Baugh explained to the Colonel how Companies F and K came to have so much, he laughed and advised company L to ask us for a division; which they asked in the way indicated, Capt, Baugh requested the companies to divide, which they cheerfully did, for we had as much as we could carry, enough to do a whole week, but as we had been on short rations about two weeks, the men packed all they could carry, eating all the time. I for one, had my haversack full, and as much as five pounds of bacon and a half bushel of crackers in a sack besides; so you see we were preparing for a long siege of short rations." 3

"That night the army camped on the mountains near Ringgold, Georgia; J.S. Thompson, P.B. Hunter and I, slept together. I on the lower side next to a pole braced against two saplings, Hunter in the middle and big, fat Jim Thompson on the upper-side. I tell you it was close sleeping, for I had to wake up Hunter and have him wake up Thompson before we could turn over; then our fire had gone out, for it was made out of dry chestnut and popped out because it was not raining, for you know chestnut will go out unless it is raining to make it pop off. Rafe, however, soon had us another fire, for he was with us. Here at Ringgold we marched through the tunnel of the mountain instead of over it, and it double file, but one man on each side of the tunnel, and this left the centre open and clear for light. We arrived back in Dalton, Georgia, without anything of interest in which Company K participated, where we finally went into winter quarters in December 1863." 3

The official report of the battle of Lookout mountain shows that it was commanded in the battle on November 24, 1863, by Lieut.-Col. A.J. Jones, and Colonel James A. Campbell being in command of the brigade picket line. Before the pickets were attacked, Jones was ordered to put his regiment in the line of battle across a bench of the mountain where they had been in bivouac, and here they were soon attacked, the enemy "seeming to force everything before them as though there was no resistance." "At close range the regiment delivered two volleys with great effect, so that the lines immediately in front broke and fell back, but the great numbers of the assaulting forces enabled them to flank the regiment and so nearly surround it that six commissioned officers and half the men were made prisoners before they could retreat. Lieut. A.V. Snowden, Company K, was killed; Lieut. Johnson, Company L, dangerously wounded and captured; Capt. Boyd, Company E, severely wounded. Col. Jones attempted to rally the remainder of the men at the ridge on the northern slope, three or four hundred yards back, but they were again outflanked and under fire at distances of eight or ten paces among the rocks at their front, and were driven back with heavy loss around the point of the mountain several hundred yards south of the Craven house, where they formed line with the rest of the brigade, and, again advancing, fought with Gen. Pettus' Alabamian's until 9 O'clock that night. The regiment was again in the fight on Missionary Ridge late in the evening of November 25, but was not exposed to the direct assault; Colonel Jones declared that the regiment never fought better, if so well, as it did on Lookout Mountain. Captain's Kennedy, Baugh, Pegg, and Boyd; Lieutenant's Brown, Bailey, and Poole; Major Welch, Hannah, and especially Lieutenant J.J. Hyde and Sgt.-Major Watkins, were commended for gallantry. Colonel Campbell and most of the picket line were cut off and captured in the first advance of the Federal line." 3 *Casualties of the regiment at Lookout Mountain 6 killed, 36 wounded, 166 missing: at Missionary Ridge, 5 wounded. 4

During this period the 27ᵗʰ Mississippi regiment and Walthall's Brigade had been assigned to Cheatham's Division, First Corps of the Army, until February 1864. 2

The records show the 27ᵗʰ Mississippi regiments' battle *casualties for all engagements around Chattanooga, totaled to 208 killed and wounded. For a time the regiment was consolidated with the 24ᵗʰ Mississippi, by December 1863 the 27ᵗʰ Mississippi's strength totally 491 men and 354 arms. 1

"Eight to ten days after the army arrived at Dalton, Georgia, after the retreat from Missionary Ridge, the army gradually went into winter quarters. I say "gradually," because axes for use in building huts were very scarce with us; about one ax to the company, so only one could build at a time. My mess having two amused servants we could work while others were getting breakfast. It would have amused you at first to see men driving boards with a pole ax, for we had no frowns until they could be made after the blacksmiths set up their forges. But quarters did not bother the men so much as short rations at first, and we began to cast about for some means to splice out our rations. Those of us who had servants and little money began to write passes for them and send them down into Georgia to get something extra for us to eat, and to sell to others. I sent Rafe and Mr. Peck sent his boy, Henry. Rafe brought back potatoes, flour and molasses, but Henry brought back ginger cakes, from Big Shanty, near Marietta. Ginger cakes sold like "hot cakes" and that settled the question as to what it would pay to buy. Mr. Peck about this time happening upon a recruit got a forty days furlough to go home. So Jim Thompson, and myself fell heir to his ginger cake trade and kept it up all winter, buying at Big Shanty where they were baked especially for us at $1.00 each for about the size of an ordinary plate and one-inch thick; we sold at $2.00 apiece at camps, upon an average of five hundred to eight hundred per week, so you see we turned a nice penny on ginger cakes, and it enabled us to get for our mess many extras that winter. Besides, Rafe brought back nearly every trip for us a bottle of apple or peach brandy and he made upon an average two trips a week, and sometimes three. Towards the last, when old Confederate money was about to go out or scaled one-third for all bills larger than five dollars, which act went into effect I think the first of April 1864, it was not uncommon thing for a man to come and buy fifty dollars' worth of ginger cake at one time to get rid of a $50 bill; he would then peddle them around for small amounts and in that way make his money. Bob Mays also kept a cake stand but his only sold when ours were out, as his were baked in large squares at an Atlanta bakery and shipped in a box to him, getting old and hard before he sold all of them. On the contrary, our cakes were always fresh, and when we had them be bought of us to eat." 3

"While here Captain W.H. Saunders was promoted to rank of Colonel and assigned to duty as Judge Advocate on Hood's Corps Court Martial. He had however been on the invalid list for some time before his promotion, and had not been with us. Here we had sent back to us from detail service, R.L. Mays, J.S. McRae, and J.B. McKinney. In a week or so after getting back to Dalton, Henry Bradford was detailed at regimental headquarters as Sergeant-Major. During this winter several of the men got twenty days furloughs to go home: T.S. Porter, J.S. Thompson, R.A, Jarman, and I think two or three others." 3

"Two or three weeks after we went into winter quarters at Dalton our brigade was detailed to do general fatigue duty with the Post Commissary, in the way of loading and unloading all cars of commissary stores that came to Dalton, and many a time it was twelve o'clock at night when we finished our day's work. But the men generally got paid in the way of sugar, coffee, and occasionally a ham, sometimes two, a sack of sweet potatoes, on the sly. The Commissary was a Mr. Denison, of the old firm of Denison & George, of Aberdeen, antebellum times. There was a guard from another brigade, but we always bribed the guard first and helped ourselves afterwards." 3

"In January, 1864, or February, we were changed from Cheatham's Division and put back in our old Hindmen's Division, Hood's Corps, and of course had to swap camps with another brigade. After that exchange we did not do regular duty at the commissary; only an occasional detail." 3

"About the middle of February there came a snow of several inches, and as there was only a wagon road of thirty feet between our brigade and Dea's Alabama brigade, we got up a snow ball fight and completely routed Dea's brigade and took possession of the camp. Then, after a truce each brigade was formed in line of battle with field officers mounted and proceeded across a creek to Managault's brigade, and another brigade of our division, routed and captured them, reformed anew and started against Stevenson's Division with a regular line of battle, skirmishers thrown out, and all, and I assure you it was rare sport that day, as charge after charge was made with only snow balls, and you could have heard the yelling and hallowing for miles. When we returned to camp the men were as tired as though we had done a sure enough day's fighting. A few days after this there were a feint made by the Federal troops and we called into line of battle, when some of the men were so foolish as to fire their quarters as they were leaving, and they repented it in a few days for we returned to the old camp . . ." 3

"During this winter, or rather in the early spring, there was organized a battalion of Sharpshooters to do away with the skirmishers. The detail from company K were first A.L. Baker and R.A. Jarman, but to keep from dividing the messes, I exchanged with A.C. Puckett, and Baker, and Puckett thence became separated from us in camp but retained on the muster roll. They were drilled separate from us and had no camp guard duty to perform." 3

"As spring began to open we were put to work on ditches and trenches in front of Dalton that were destined to never be used by us, but to perfect us in something that was to bear a prominent part in the campaign of 1864." 3

"Between the 20th of April 1864 and the first of May, we broke up our winter quarters and moved out to the front and went into camp (using the boards off of our quarters to make shelters) to insure us to the hardships of the coming campaign. While here several of the men had fights with one another for some trivial causes, but they soon made up again, as it was against their nature to stay mad long at the time, besides the other men made all manner of fun of them, and said the spring fights had opened, and wanting to know when they might expect the next round, as they wanted to have skirmishers thrown out and bring it on in grand style, and it would always end in a laugh and make up." 3

"Several times while in camp we were called on to go in support of the cavalry, and we were frequently in line of battle but no fighting, although we could hear skirmishing at times in the distance. I recollect on one occasion in front of Dalton, while out supporting cavalry, we came across a large pile of knapsacks that had been piled up and for some cause abandoned by the Federal infantry. Here we supplied ourselves with new oil cloths, and sections of small tents that were of great service to us." 3

"We finally retreated back to "Resaca," where we had a hard contested fight on the 15 and 16 of May, the first real battle of the Georgia campaign. I do not remember who was hurt here, except J.W. Peck wounded in the hip, and myself, bruised from a spent ball on the shin. It was hot here, for the Federal line in our immediate front was not over 150 yards off, and they could use their rifles with fatal effect; but we did our best, and I think succeeded in paying them back in kind. Here in the midst of companies F and K, Lieutenant-Colonel Jones, of the 27th Mississippi regiment, was killed by a sharpshooter at an old house in our front, but the artillery soon fired it, and we made it very hot for them there with our rifles. The Federals came near pushing us out of our position the first day by firing the woods in our front, and the leaves setting fire to our temporary rail breast works, but that night we put dirt the rails, and did not stand in so much dread the second day. After dark on the night of the 16th of May, we withdrew our lines and fell back, and made no very important stand until on the evening of May 25th, at New Hope church. Although we did no fighting ourselves, we were in the first or second line of reserves and under fire part of the time, and stray shots falling most of the time." 3

"If my recollection serves me right, there were some four or five lines of Mississippi troops in reserve, but the brave Georgians in front were fighting for homes, and loved ones they could see fleeing from the invaders and their burning homes (for it was said that two companies in that line were mustered into service, and lived around "New Hope church") and they only needed encouragement, and to know that help was near, and how well did next day reveal how they used their rifles, from the numbers of slain in their front. Here, this night, after the battle was over, we met many of our old friends and neighbors that had just joined Johnson's Army with Loring's Division from Mississippi. During the next to days, while our lines were getting established, and we were in reserve, on the 27th of May we, with Granbury's Texas brigade, were double-quick to our right to support some cavalry, when, before we could form and close up, faced to the front and in not more than two or three volleys almost annihilated a line of Federal infantry, in some places, and in not more than ten to twenty steps from us, for their guns were empty from chasing cavalry, and they had no idea that a line of infantry was in half a mile from them. In that engagement the Confederate infantry lost only about four or five men. It was said at the next day about seven hundred federals were buried from that engagement and some two hundred prisoners taken that night. Next day, May 28th, we were chasing around in support of cavalry, and late that evening rejoined our division. Several days were spent here in line of battle, when we were again forced to retreat and did it at night, and it was as dark and rainy a night as you would wish to see; and next morning we were all muddy and wet and mad. During the night one of the company, Jim Thompson, I believe stopped in a branch to get some water, after he had taken his drink he found he was standing on a dead horse or mule, and not on a log; but a soldier stomach were too strong for that, and he laughed many a time afterwards about it. We were in all the engagements with our division and corps." 3

"In from of Marietta, Lost Mountain and at Kennesaw Mountain we had close and dangerous picket duty to perform, and each man was required to carry 80 rounds of ammunition on picket with him, stand four hours at a time and keep up a lively shooting all the time, particularly during the day, and on some of our picket posts the Yankee sharpshooters kept things too hot and lively for a man to get lonesome. There was a North Carolina regiment to our left on the Kennesaw line, and one night I heard a Yankee call over to Johnnie Reb to know what regiment it was on duty there, when he was answered some North Carolina, they, the Yankee, wanted to know if Johnnie Reb had any tobacco to swap for coffee, when answered in the negative, the Yankee asked what he had to swap; Johnnie Reb replied, some of the best rosin he had ever closed his teeth over, then there was a grand laugh on both sides. Many amusing incidents happened all along there, that I cannot remember now while writing, but they frequently come up when I have no means of taking them down. Some time soon after we left the Kennesaw Mountain line, or about the time we left, I one evening saw a duel between two Yankee batteries. At first the one took the other for a Confederate battery, and they put it to each other hot for some time; and during this engagement between the batteries we had to change sides of our breast works, for we found the front safer than behind them, We finally fell back to the line of works being erected north of the Chattahoochee River from Atlanta, and went to work to strengthen them, and the negroes at work on them were sent back towards Atlanta." 3

"After occupying these lines for a short time, the army fell back across the Chattahoochee River, when it was said that we would rest for a few days, Gen. Johnson being relieved and Gen. Hood put in command of the army, and Gen. S.D. Lee in command of our corps. About this time too, there was an election ordered in Company K, for Third Lieutenant, as Lt. McMillan was prisoner of war and Second Lieutenant, no one could be promoted over him. A.C. Powell was elected Lieutenant. During all this campaign Col. W.F. Brantley, of the 29th Mississippi regiment, had been in command of the brigade, and Gen. Walthall promoted to command of a division; Gen. Hindman was our division commander. About this time, or shortly after, Col. Brantley was promoted to Brigadier General, and our brigade was known as Brantley's brigade thereafter." 3

ORDER OF BATTLE CONFEDERATE FORCES			
NORTHERN GEORGIA CAMPAIGN - BATTLES OF CHATTANOOGA			
NOVEMBER 23-25, 1863			
ARMY OF TENNESSEE - C.S.A.			
Commanding: General Braxton Bragg			
40,000 Men			
LONGSTREET'S CORPS: LEFT WING/			
Commanding: Lt.Gen. James Longstreet			
	MC LAWS'S DIVISION:		
	Commanding: Brig.Gen. Joseph B. Kershaw		
		KERSHAW'S BRIGADE:	
			(5 S.C. Regts)
		HUMPHREY'S BRIGADE:	
			(4 Mississippi Regts)
		WOOFFORD'S BRIGADE:	
			(3 Ga Regts; 2 Ga Legions)
		BRYAN'S BRIGADE:	
			(4 Georgia Regts)
	HOOD'S DIVISION:		
	Commanding: Brig.Gen. E. Mc Iver Law		
		LAW'S BRIGADE:	
			(5 Alabama Regts)
		ROBERTSON'S BRIGADE:	
			(3 Texas Regts; 1 Ark Regt; 1 Ga Regt)
		JENKIN'S BRIGADE:	
			(4 S.C. Regts; 1 S.C. Legion)
		BENNING'S BRIGADE:	
			(4 Georgia Regts)
HARDEE'S CORPS:			
Commanding: Lt.Gen. William Hardee			
	(First) CHEATHAM'S DIVISION:		
	Commanding: Maj.Gen. Benjamin F. Cheatham		
		JACKSON'S BRIGADE:	
			(4 Georgia Regts; 1 Mississippi Regt)

		3rd (Anderson's/Walthall's) BRIGADE:	
		Commanding: Brig.Gen. Edward C. Walthall	
			24th Mississippi
			27th Mississippi (Consl)
			29th-30th Mississippi
			30th Mississippi
		1st (Donelson's/Wright's) BRIGADE:	
			(6 Tennessee Regts)
		MOORE'S BRIGADE:	
			(3 Alabama Regts)
	SECOND (Wither's/Hindman's) DIVISION:		
	Commanding: Maj.Gen. Thomas C. Hindman		
		1st (Loomis/Deas') BRIGADE:	
			(6 Alabama Regts)
		2nd (Chalmer'sAnderson's) BRIGADE:	
			(5 Mississippi Regts)
		4th (Manigualt's) BRIGADE:	
			(3 Alabama Regts; 2 S.C. Regts)
		(Smith's/Vaughan's) BRIGADE:	
			(6 Tennessee Regts)
	BUCKNER'S DIVISION:		
	Commanding: Maj.Gen. Buckner		
		3rd (Johnson's) BRIGADE:	
			(5 Tennessee Regts; 1 CSA Regt)
		GRACIE'S BRIGADE:	
			(2 Alabama Regts; 1 Alabama Legion)
		REYNOLD'S BRIGADE:	
			(2 N.C. Regts; 2 Va Regts)
	WALKER'S DIVISION:		
	Commanding: Maj.Gen. Walker		
		3rd (Maney) BRIGADE:	
			(8 Tennessee Regt)
		GIST'S BRIGADE:	
			(2 S.C. Regts; 1 Georgia Regt)
		WILSON'S BRIGADE:	
			(3 Georgia Regts)

BRECKINRIDGE'S ARMY CORPS:			
	Commanding: Lt.Gen. John C. Breckinridge		
	CLEBURN'S DIVISION:		
	Commanding: Maj.Gen. Patrick Cleburn		
		LIDDELL'S BRIGADE:	
			(9 Arkansas Regts)
		POLK'S BRIGADE:	
			(3 Tenn Regts; 1 Ark Regt; 2 CSA Regts)
		SMITH'S BRIGADE:	
			(8 Texas Regts)
		LOWERY'S BRIGADE:	
			(3 Alabama Regts; 2 Mississippi Regts)
	STEWART'S DIVISION:		
	Commanding: Maj.Gen. Alexander P. Stewart		
		ADAM'S BRIGADE:	
			(5 Louisiana Regts)
		STRAHL'S BRIGADE:	
			(5 Tennessee Regts)
		CLAYTON'S BRIGADE:	
			(4 Alabama Regts)
		STOVALL'S BRIGADE:	
			(4 Georgia Regts)
	BRECKINRIDGE'S DIVISION:		
	Commanding: Lt.Gen. John C. Breckinridge		
		LEWIS'S BRIGADE:	
			(5 Kentucky Regts)
		BATE'S BRIGADE:	
			(5 Tennessee Regts; 1 Georgia Regt)
	STEVESON'S DIVISION:		
	Commanding: Maj.Gen. C. Stevenson		
		BROWN'S BRIGADE:	
			(6 Tennessee Regts)
		CUMMING'S BRIGADE:	
			(4 Georgia Regts)
		PETIS'S BRIGADE:	

			(5 Alabama Regts)
		VAUGHAN'S BRIGADE:	
			(4 Tennessee Regts)

WHEELER CAV CORPS:

Commanding: Maj.Gen.Joseph Wheeler

	MARTIN'S CAV DIVISION:		
	Commanding: Maj.Gen. William Martin		
		1st CAV BRIGADE:	
			(2 Tex Regts; 1 Ark Regt; 1 N.C. Regt)
		2nd CAV BRIGADE:	
			(5 Tennessee Regts)

	ARMSTRONG'S DIVISION:		
	Commanding: Brig.Gen. William Martin		
		1st CAV BRIGADE:	
			(5 Tennessee Regts)
		2nd CAV BRIGADE:	
			(4 Bns)

	KELLEY'S CAV DIVISION:		
	Commanding: Col. W. Wade		
		1st CAV BRIGADE:	
			(4 CSA Regts)
		2nd CAV BRIGADE:	
			(3 Kentucky Regts; 1 Legion)

		RODDEY'S CAV BRIGADE:	
			(3 Alabama Regts- Detached Svc)

Re: Bush, Bryan S; The Civil War Battles of the Western Theater; 1998; Pgs 65-66

CHATTANOOGA, TENNESSEE 1863

RE: THE CIVIL WAR OF THE WESTERN THEATER
M

PART TWO

THE VALOROUS DEFENSE . . . !!

THE GEORGIA CAMPAIGN

The Northern Georgia Campaign and Battling for Dalton, Resaca, New Hope and Ezra Church near Atlanta . . . .

CHAPTER VIII.

ATLANTA, GEORGIA: MAY 1864.

In the Atlanta Campaign, Walthall's Brigade was part of Hindmen's Division, commanded by Gen. John C. Brown and Gen. Patton Anderson, in Hood's Corps, after July 27 commanded by Gen. S.D. Lee. General Walthall was promoted to command a division in June, and Colonel Benton commanded the brigade until Brig.-Gen. Brantley was promoted. 1

The Twenty-seventh began the campaign joined with the Twenty-fourth under Colonel Benton, was soon succeeded by Lieut.-Col. McKelvaine. They were on the entrenched line at Alt's Gap, May 7, and on May 14-15 engaged in the battle of "Resaca," where the brigade was distinguished for the gallant defense of a position exposed to an enfilading fire of artillery as well as the assault of infantry which was repulsed in front. Lieut.-Col. A.J. Jones and Capt. J.R. Poole fell, instantly killed in the battle line. In all there were 6 killed and 27 wounded." 4 & 1

The brigade was not seriously engaged at Cassville, New Hope, or Kennesaw Mountain, through skirmishing was constant, nor in the battle around Atlanta, until July 28, when McClain's command advanced on the Lickskillet road, driving the enemy from the hill. When moving by the right flank, a Federal attack was made which threw the command into temporary confusion. Here (at "Ezra Church") McKelvaine was severely wounded, and Lieut.-Col. W.L. Lyles took command. The two regiments had 430 in battle: 11 killed, 67 wounded, 10 of whom were left on the field. 1 The Twenty-seventh served in the trenches on the west side of Atlanta (see Fourth Regiment) until August 30, when they marched to meet Sherman's flank movement, and went into battle at Jonesboro, where the brigade suffered heavy losses in a frontal attack upon the Federal entrenched line. The Twenty-seventh had 4 killed and 23 wounded. Capt. J.R. Baugh, commanding the regiment was mortally wounded; Adjutant J.L. Bufkin, Capt. S.M. Pegg, Capt. J.H. Wood, Lieutenant's. J.J. Jarman and William Welch severely wounded. 4

ORDER OF BATTLE CONFEDERATE FORCES			
CENTRAL GEORGIA CAMPAIGN - BATTLE OF ATLANTA			
JUNE - AUGUST 31, 1864			
ARMY OF MISSISSIPPI - C.S.A.			
Acting Commanding: Maj.Gen. William B. Loring			
17,000 Men			
LORING'S DIVISION: RIGHT WING			
	Commanding: Maj.Gen. Loring		
		1st (Featherson's) BRIGADE:	
			(5 Mississippi Regts)
		2nd (Adams) BRIGADE:	
			(6 Mississippi Regts)
		3rd (Scott) BRIGADE:	
			(5 Ala Regts; 1 La Regt)
FRENCH'S DIVISION:			
	Commanding: Maj.Gen. Samuel French		
		1st (Ector) BRIGADE:	
			(2 N.C. Regts; 4 Tex Regts)
		2nd (Cockrell) BRIGADE:	
			(8 Missouri Regts)
		3rd (Sears) BRIGADE:	
			(5 Mississippi Regts)
CANTEY'S DIVISION:			
	Commanding: Brig.Gen. James Cantey		
		1st (Reynold's) BRIGADE:	
			(5 Arkansas Regts)
		2nd (Murphy's) BRIGADE:	
			(4 Alabama Regts)
		3rd (Quarles) BRIGADE:	
			(7 Alabama Regts)
ARMY OF TENNESSEE - C.S.A.			
Commander: General Joseph E. Johnston			
45,000 Men			
HARDEE'S CORPS:			

	Commanding: Lt.Gen.William Hardee		
(First CHEATHAM'S DIVISION:			
	Commanding: Maj.Gen. Benjamin F. Cheatham		
		MANEY'S BRIGADE:	
			(8 Tennessee Regts)
		1st (Donelson's) WRIGHTS BRIGADE:	
			(6 Tennessee Regts)
		STRAHL'S BRIGADE:	
			(6 Tennessee Regts)
		(Smith's) VAUGHAN'S BRIGADE:	
			(6 Tennessee Regts)
CLEBURN'S DIVISION:			
	Commanding: Maj.Gen. Patrick Cleburn		
		(Liddell's) GOVAN'S BRIGADE:	
			(7 Arkansas Regts; 1 CSA Regt)
		POLK'S BRIGADE:	
			(2 Ark Regts; 3 Tenn Regts; 1 CSA Regt)
		GRANBURY'S BRIGADE:	
			(7 Texas Regts)
		SMITH'S BRIGADE:	
			(4 Georgia Regts)
		LOWERY'S BRIGADE:	
			(2 Miss Regts; 3 Ala Regts; 3 Ark Regts)
HINDMAN'S DIVISION:			
	Commanding:		
		WALTHALL'S BRIGADE:	
		Commanding: Col. S. Benson	
			24th Mississippi
			27th Mississippi (Consl 24th)
			29th-30th Mississippi
			30th Mississippi
			34th Mississippi
		DEA'S BRIGADE:	
		2nd (Chalmer'sAnderson's) TUCKER'S BRIGADE:	
			(5 Mississippi Regts)
		4th MANIGAULT'S BRIGADE:	
			(3 Alabama Regts; 2 S.C. Regts)

WALKER'S DIVISION:			
	Commanding: Maj.Gen. Walker		
		MERCER'S BRIGADE:	
			(Unknown Regts)
		JACKSON'S BRIGADE:	
			(4 Georgia Regts; 1 Mississippi Regt)
		GIST'S BRIGADE:	
			(2 Ga Regts; 2 Miss Regts; 2 S.C. Regts)
		(Wilson's) STEVEN'S BRIGADE:	
			(5 Georgia Regts)
STEVESON'S DIVISION:			
	Commanding:		
		BROWN'S BRIGADE:	
			(6 Tennessee Regts)
		CUMMING'S BRIGADE:	
			(5 Georgia Regts)
		PETTIS'S BRIGADE:	
			(5 Alabama Regts)
		REYNOLD'S BRIGADE:	
			(2 N.C. Regts; 2 Va Regts)
STEWART'S DIVISION:			
	Commanding: Maj.Gen. Alexander Stewart		
		STOVALL'S BRIGADE:	
			(5 Georgia Regts)
		GIBSON BRIGADE:	
			(8 Louisiana Regts)
		BAKER'S BRIGADE:	
			(4 Alabama Regts)
		CLAYTON'S BRIGADE:	
			(5 Alabama Regts)
HOOD'S DIVISION:			
	Commanding: Brig.Gen. E. Mc Iver Law		
		LAW'S BRIGADE:	
			(5 Alabama Regts)
		ROBERTSON'S BRIGADE:	
			(1 Ark Regt; 3 Tex Regts; 1 Ga Regt)

		JENKIN'S BRIGADE:	
			(5 S.C. Regts)
		BENNING'S BRIGADE:	
			(4 Georgia Regts)

FIRST GEORGIA MILITIA DIVISION:	
Commanding: Maj.Gen. Gustavus Smith	

		1st BRIGADE:	
			(5 Ga R.M.)
		2nd BRIGADE:	
			(3 Ga R.M.)
		3rd BRIGADE:	
			(3 Ga R.M.)
		4th BRIGADE:	
			(3 Ga R.M.)

WHEELER CAV CORPS:
Commanding: Maj.Gen.Joseph Wheeler

MARTIN'S CAV DIVISION:	
	Commanding: Maj.Gen. William Martin

		1st CAV BRIGADE:	
			(1 Ark Regt; 1 N.C. Regt; 2 Tex Regts)
		2nd CAV BRIGADE:	
			(5 Tennessee Regts)

(Armstrong's) MARTIN'S DIVISION:	
	Commanding: Brig.Gen. William Martin

		ALLEN'S BRIGADE:	
			(5 Alabama Regts)
		IVERSON'S BRIGADE:	
			(5 Georgia Regts)

KELLEY'S CAV DIVISION:	
	Commanding: Brig.Gen. J. H. Kelley

		1st CAV DIBRELL'S BRIGADE:	
			(5 Tennessee Regts)
		1st CAV ANDERSON'S BRIGADE:	
			(4 CSA Regts; 1 Ga Regt)

		HANNON'S CAV BRIGADE:	
			(2 Ala Regts; 1 Kentucky Regt)
HUME'S DIVISION:			
	Commanding: Brig.Gen. W. Humes		
		ASHBY'S CAV BRIGADE:	
			(3 Tennessee Regts)
		HARRISON'S BRIGADE:	
			(1 Ark Regt; 1 Tenn Regt; 2 Tex Regts)
		2nd CAV GRIGSBY'S BRIGADE:	
			(4 Kentucky Regts)
Re:Bush, Bryan S.; The Civil War Battles of the Western Theater; 1998; Pgs 74-77.			

NORTH-CENTRAL GEORGIA, 1863

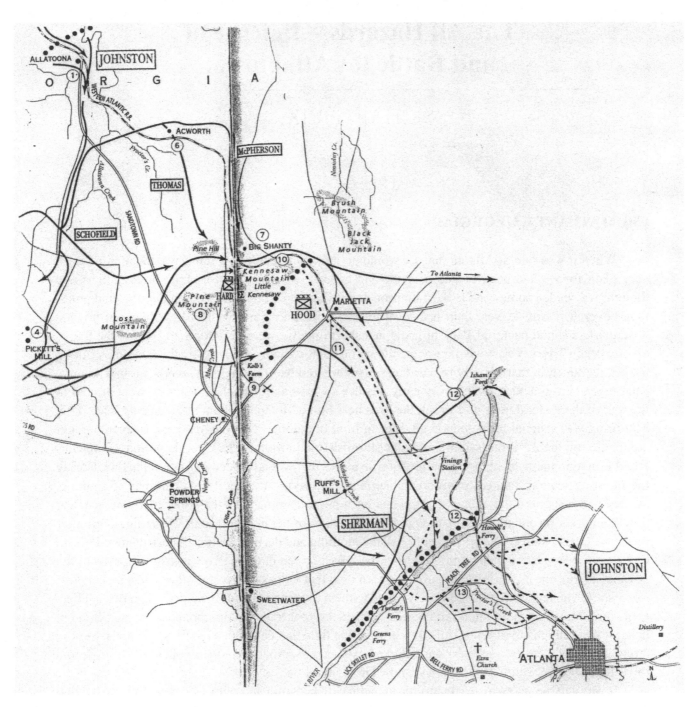

RE: THE CIVIL WAR OF THE WESTERN THEATER
M

The All Hazards—Defense of
and Battle for Atlanta . . .

CHAPTER IX.

City of ATLANTA, GEORGIA:

"When it was said at Atlanta that we would go into camp and rest a few days, the men were all very glad, for we had been in line of battle and under fire of artillery for about three months and thought we needed some rest. H.S. Thompson and I, fixed up a bunk to sleep on out of round poles, then covered it with leaves, then lay down to rest. In a short time we heard the bugle at brigade headquarters sound pack up! Pack up! And in a short time we were in motion, to support the troops up on "Peach Tree Creek." We did not go into battle but the enemy's lines were thick at times among us. We remained in that vicinity two or three days then fell back to the inside works around Atlanta. That night, or the next morning very early, Hardee's Corps and Wheeler's Cavalry went around to the rear of the Federal lines and struck the lines near Stone Mountain about noon on July 22d, 1864. The firing was a signal for a general advance in front of the line. That day there were seven or eight companies on the 27th Mississippi put on the skirmish line in front of the Georgia militia, companies F and K among them, to support a battery of rifle pieces that was advanced in front of the line. During the morning several Yankees came in and surrendered, saying they preferred captivity to fighting, as they had just heard that General Hood had been put in command of the Army of Tennessee, and they knew that meant fighting. Although the battle did not begin on our part of the line until after twelve O'clock, we were under picket fire all the morning and during the morning Lieutenant Powell, of Company K was wounded and died from the effects in ten days or two weeks afterwards. In the advance of our line as skirmishers through a corn field that day I shot several times into a picket post; I saw some Yankees dodge in and finally called to them to come out and surrender, when two soldiers came out holding up their hands, and when I reached the post found an officer and a private behind it, dead; it was only made of fence rails. I went from the field that day with a batch of prisoners, back to Atlanta, turned over the prisoners and returned. About sunset that night we rejoined the brigade and the brigade took position held that day by the Georgia militia." 3

"It was very amusing to see the militia in battle with bed quilt and pillows and packs large enough for a mule. No old soldier would have carried such a load—he would have thrown it away. While here, part of our company, helped by the artillery company near by, killed a large bull one night, and we had fresh beef a day or two. My pocket knife went with the crowd to kill the bull though I did not, but I received my share of the beef." 3

"We remained on that part of the line until July 28th, 1864, when we were moved to the opposite side of Atlanta, in quick time, to the Lick Skilled road, and that evening we had hard fighting and heavy losses. There were two file closers shot behind me that day—J.S. McRae, across the shoulder, slight wound, and one of Company K shot in the chin. Here T.A. Benner and James H. Dean were wounded and never rejoined us again. If any of Company K were killed that day I do not now recollect it. We lost Major Kennedy, of the 27th Mississippi, and Lieutenant-Colonel McKelvaine, of the 24th Mississippi, and our commanding officer, was wounded, so he never joined us again. Captain Baugh, of company F, 27th Mississippi being our senior Captain now had charge of the regiment as he was ranking officer and had stood examination for the rank of Colonel, as Colonel Campbell had died in prison. For the next few days we had fighting everyday for position, both sides wanting the advantage, which finally culminated in the Federal charging our picket lines on August 3rd. That day the 34th Mississippi reinforced the 27th Mississippi and retook them. They reinforced and again charged just after a hard rain before we had time to dry our guns and it was hard fighting the balance of the day, part of the line in our brigade using the bayonet and clubbing the musket. After we retook the picket line as first it forced from six to eight men in picket holes only intended for two, and being short of ammunition the officer of the day did not like to make a detail. As it was a very hazardous undertaking to run out from the picket line he visited several holes and called for volunteers. I for one volunteered to make the run, and we had a pass under fire for two hundred yards to get out. It was a dangerous undertaking but I considered my chances in running and staying, concluding that running out for ammunition was safer that remaining in a crowded picket hole and it in the range of artillery. I made the run out safe, and when I returned I found two wounded and one killed out of five I left in the picket hole, and later in the day the other two were captured, one of whom was T.S. Porter, of Co. K, so you see that time a good run was better than a bad stand." 3

"That night we established new picket lines and began to ditch towards each other and when about the last week in August the Federal line fell back and flanked us out of Atlanta. I stepped the distance between the picket lines, and found it to be only eighteen steps from outside to outside of picket lines in front of our brigade. While in such close quarters there were several men wounded and some killed. R.C. Jones, of Company K was wounded. Nearly all the wounded were shot in the head—so that most the wounds were fatal." 3

"Our line of battle was well entrenched with earthworks and in front of them brush and stakes drove into the ground at an angle of forty-five degrees, with grape vines worked in and through them; then more brush and stakes, for some seventy-five or one hundred yards, with a narrow road though for the pickets to pass, and that well guarded. The men called the brush "tangle foot," and the stakes "haver-sack stealers." If the Federals had undertaken to charge, it would have certainly been tangle foot for them. While in line here, about the middle of August, we had another election for Third Lieutenant to succeed Lieutenant Powell, who had died from wounds; J.J. Inman was this time elected." 3

"I think we left East Fort, ncck Atlanta, when flanked by the Federals on the evening of August 30th, and after an all night march we arrived about noon at "Jonesboro," Georgia, where that evening we had one of the hardest fought battles of the campaign. We that evening charged the Federals in their breast works, though a field, and coming to a fence row, some thirty or forty steps from the Federal line, our line halted to rest, and it was fatal to them, for never did they advance again, but were shot down and completely routed. Company K, here lost A.L. Baker, killed; Lieutenant J.J. Inman, wounded and died; H.V. White, wounded and sent to the hospital, and R.L. Mays and J.S. Thompson, both slightly; J.S. Thompson being saved by a knife in his pocket, which was broken all to pieces, and caused the ball to glance, making a slight wound on the hip. We ditched all night preparing for an attack next day, but about daylight, we sent our tools back to the wagons and started back to Atlanta to guard our wagon train and the artillery left there. We met it late that evening coming out and went on guard, or rather formed a picket line and let the train pass on. Next morning we come in as rear guard, but kept a skirmish line out at the road side and parallel to the road, and I think had to form line of battle once or twice, but no engagement occurred. We went out by the way of McDonald, and arrived at the army at a little place near Jonesboro, where, after a few days skirmishing and picket duty, we went into camp to rest for a few days. While doing picket duty here, one day Bob Mayes, of Company K, and others of the regiment, were out on a scout between the two armies, when they captured a Yankee in a field of corn after roasting ears, and they also killed a nice hog-that gave us pork, and to keep us from cooking it, orders were issued to have no fires built until further orders. The second day after, Rafe came to us and we all sent our pork off to be cooked, and before we got it back all the brigade had fires and were cooking their meat." 3

"While encamped near Jonesboro, Georgia, we were mustered and had to make out new muster roll for Company K, I improvised a desk to write on, out of round strait poles, and covered it with my blanket, then with my oil cloth, when I had a fairly good desk (we used the same for a dinning table), I succeeded in getting my roll right the first time, then making two copies. I helped several other companies to right their rolls, for our mustering officer on that occasion was Capt. Joe Ward, Company L, 24th Mississippi, and also of Aberdeen, and he was very strict." 3

"There in two or three days after going into camp, orders came from brigade headquarters for the men to be drilled two hours in the morning and same in the evening, but the privates and non-commissioned officers of the 24th and 27th Mississippi regiments refused, and every man went to his tent and lay down, and when orders were given to the 29th and 30th Mississippi regiments if they attempted to arrest us, the 34th Mississippi regiment joined us, and every man loaded his gun and lay down by it, but sent word to the 29th and 30th regiments if they attempted to arrest us they might expect a fight, and as a matter of course they made no arrests. We began to drill, or at least went out to drill in a day or two. For this all non-commissioned officers were reduced one rank, but it did not in the least affect Company K, for she had none, either commissioned or non-commissioned for Lieutenant J.J. Inman died of his wounds received at Jonesboro. While here was a flag of truce sent between the two armies, and with it was sent the effects of Capt. Baugh, Company F, rather Col. Baugh, 27th Mississippi, as he was wounded and captured at Jonesboro, and died in the hands of the Federals, but being a Mason, he fell in good and true brother Masons, and they sent every dollar of money he had, even his pocket knife and a letter addressed to his mother he had written before he died, all packed together, to care of Company F, 27th Mississippi. How long we stayed there I do not remember, but I remember Gen. S.D. Lee, our Corps commander, having each division of the corps marched out to an old field one day, and after forming by divisions into squares, he made a speech to us, and in that speech he said that Hardee's corps could charge and take breast works, and he was determined that his corps should do as much, and he wanted them to understand and act accordingly." 3

"I do not now recollect how long we stayed here, but our next move was when General Hood started to the rear of Sherman at Atlanta. We went across to a little town then deserted, or rather moved on the Atlanta & West Point railroad to Newman. While here two Monroe county men came to see us one morning, Ira G. Holloway and James Holloway, and when we asked them to stay for dinner with us, they consented if it did not deprive us of our rations, and when assured it would not, they cheerfully accepted the invitation. The day before Bob Mayes, while scouting between lines, brought a bee gum and helped to kill a hog; but the Federal cavalry run them off the hog once, but they went back and got it again, and that morning my servant, Rafe, had come in with about a half bushel of biscuits ready baked and some butter, so you ought to have seen us trying to put on style to our guests. Mr. Ira Holloway said when he saw the spread that it was more than he had seen one mess have since he had been in the army, but he had just come to the army. Our next move from here, I think, was to near Marietta, Georgia, and while there two of Company K, who I will call Allen and Butler, as both are now living in Monroe county on the east side of the river, for fear of hurting their feelings, (Allen and Butler are true given names) came to me one evening, as I was then acting Orderly Sergeant, and said if I would manage to excuse them a while from fatigue duty on breast works we were building there, they would give me some mutton, and being a deer lover of mutton, I arranged to let them go, with some four or five others. After being gone some hour or more, the detail sneaking back, muddy and wet and no mutton; but it soon leaked out that instead of sheep they had seen, it was where the beef of some division had been slaughtered and the paunches had been left, and from a distance it looked like a flock of sheep lying down. I will not say which members of Company K was said to have shot a paunch and then jumped on it with a knife, but suffice to say they had to stop at the branch and wash, and they were a crestfallen set. All the rest of the war we would holler at them every time we would pass a slaughter pen to come up and draw their mutton; we missed our mutton, but had a heap of fun. After leaving the line formed near Marietta, Georgia, we bore to the left and went south to Rome, Georgia, and crossed the Coosa River at a little place called Coosaville. On the march one evening we came to a large creek across the road and lane on one side of the creek we were on, and the division was put in double column, one on each side of the road and the men all ordered to pull off shoes and pants to wade the creek, which at the ford was about two and a half feet deep probably three feet, and just as the head of the column started to ford the creek, along came two ladies in a buggy and had to face a whole division of men in their shirt tails, and the whoop that went up along the lines as they passed through could have been heard fully one mile. We filed to our right as soon as we crossed the creek and camped on the banks; that night my mess had slap jacks and molasses for supper. Next day just before we got to the Coosa River we passed in the evening a little school house near the road, and as we passed there were two girls, or young ladies, and one boy sitting in the door of the school house and singing as our bare-footed squad came by. That night we camped at Coosaville, Bob Mayes was detailed to guard a sweet potato patch, and when I carried supper to him he had near a bushel ready for me, so that next day we had plenty of roasted potatoes. Next morning, I think it was, that the bare-footed squad were ordered to the slaughter pen, and there got fresh raw hide to make moccasins, out of, and to turn the hair side in; the boys said that they felt comfortable at first, but when they got hot and dry they hurt the feet, and as a matter of course were then thrown away, but renewed each morning." 3

"Our objective point now was Resaca, Georgia, and when we arrived in front of the place the Federals held the position we had in May, and we occupied their position, but we did not charge the works as they had, we simply held them there while the other part of the army tore up the railroad to Dalton, and captured the stockades near Dalton, held by negro troops, that being done, we filled the gap in the mountain with timber to keep from being pursued too fast by cavalry or artillery, when we turned southwest for Gadsden, Alabama, for supplies." 3

According to official records, "Thence they moved to Gadsden, Ala., and crossed the Tennessee River on the last days of October, (1864)." 4

Alabama: "We stayed at Gadsden only a day or two, but left there hurriedly in the evening, with our three days rations only half cooked. We carried our meat, of course, but the bread stuff was corn meal dough, and had to be thrown away. Next day at 12 O'clock my mess ate up the last of our three days rations, and as we were then on Sand Mountain, it looked gloomy, or as the boys expressed it, starvation stared us in the face as big as a ten acre field. But thanks again to Rafe, he got us a large turkey gobbler and about thirty pounds of flour and a canteen of sorghum, and I with some other men on a scout for something to eat, got the shoulder of a fresh killed hog, skinned as a matter of course. We cooked the pork and some biscuit that night, dressed the gobbler and carried him all next day and roasted him that night at the foot of Sand Mountain, while Bob Mayes again got more potatoes to eat with the turkey gravy that we caught while baking in our tin plates. We went on in the direction of Decatur, Alabama, but the command did not go through Decatur, but were close enough to hear firing there. We struck the Memphis & Charleston railroad between Decatur and Oburtland, and followed the railroad to Leighton. Just before we got to Leighton, about four miles, I got a good food supply for my mess in bacon and biscuits. We camped for the night at Leighton, but early next morning we started in the direction of Florence, Alabama, and that evening we crossed the Tennessee River by ferriage in some pontoon boats, above Florence where there is an island in the river. We ferried to the island, pulled our boats across the island and ferried the other prong of the river. General Sharp's brigade with our division commander, Gen. Edward Johnson, preceded us. While the 27th Mississippi was in the boats the Federal cavalry began to fire on Gen. Sharp's brigade and a few stray shots at us, but Sharp's brigade soon captured the detachment of cavalry sent against us, and that night we camped in Florence, but it was late when we got there, as it was dark before all of our brigade crossed over. We did picket and guard duty around Florence for some two weeks, and nearly everyday or night for part of the time had skirmishing with Federal Cavalry. Finally, when the drift and high water in the Tennessee River permitted the army to keep up its pontoon bridge, the main army crossed over and rations became more plentiful. Our division was sent out to where the Huntsville road crossed Shoal Creek, and early one morning Sharp's brigade waded over and got behind a brigade of Federal Cavalry and routed them and captured part of their commissary stores giving us for a few days good fat beef. We continued on picket along Shoal Creek until the army commenced its advance into Tennessee. While here on Shoal Creek the men frequently waded over under the cover of our rifles and gathered corn to bring back with them to a mill on our side of the creek and have it ground. The corn and mill belonged to the same man, but he said he rather the Confederates had it than the Federals, and besides he got the toll out of it, which if the Federals got it he lost. While out here, we had clothing issued to us at the following very cheap rates for jean jackets and pants: Drawers, $3.00; pants, $12.00; jackets, $14.00; shoes, $10.00; socks, $1.00; blankets, $10.00; shirt, $3.00; wool hat, $5.00; cap, $2.00. For the last six or eight weeks I had been acting Orderly Sergeant, as there was not a non-commissioned officer in our consolidated company. While on Shoal Creek we got from the fields near us plenty of peas, but they had to get after dark." 3

Brantley's Brigade shared the operations of Lee's Corps during the October, 1864, campaign against Chattanooga & Atlanta railway, the investment of Resaca and holding the Snake Creek gap against Sherman's army while Hood retreated behind mountains. Brantley's men were engaged in sharp skirmishing at the gap on October 15. 4

Official records indicated the regiment moved to Gadsden, Alabama and thence, the Tennessee River on the last days of October (1864). The division under the command on Maj.-Gen. Edward Johnson, advanced with Lee's Corps to Columbia, and was then taken, November 29, by General Hood, to assist in the rear attack at Spring Hill. 4

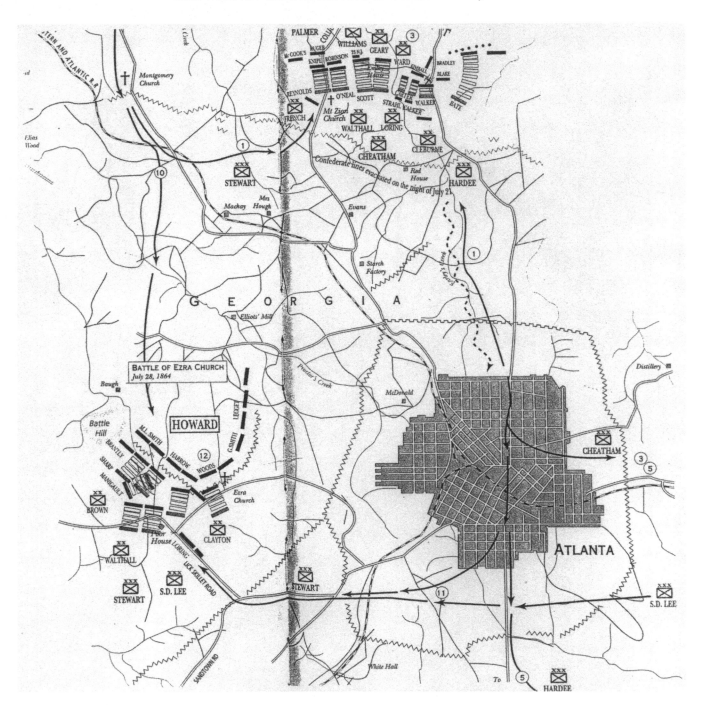

RE: THE CIVIL WAR OF THE WESTERN THEATER

SOUTH ATLANTA AND JONESBORO, GEORGIA 1864

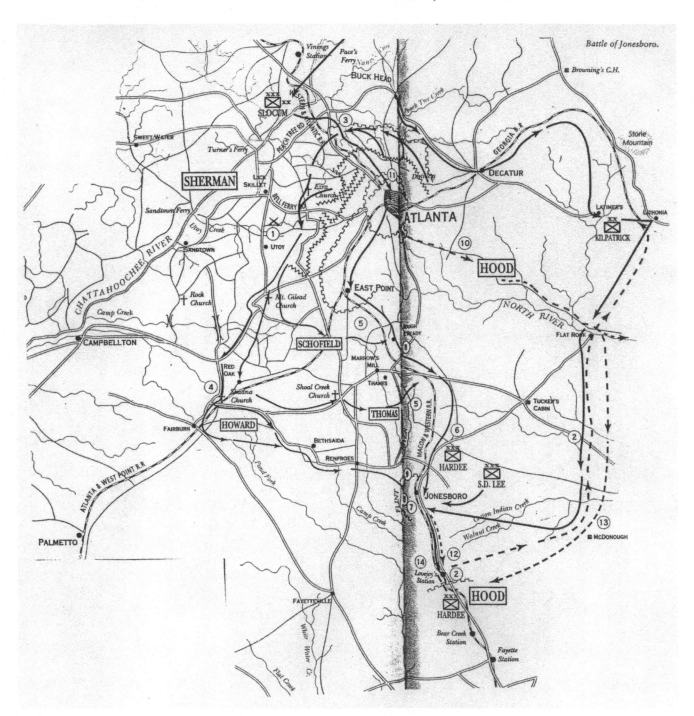

RE: THE CIVIL WAR OF THE WESTERN THEATER
RE: ILLUSTRATED ATLAS OF THE CIVIL WAR
M

The Second Central Tennessee Campaign—
Invasion, and the Battle for Franklin . . .

CHAPTER X.

FRANKLIN, TENNESSEE: NOVEMBER 1864.

Tennessee: "We left our position on Shoal Creek, near Florence, Alabama, where we were doing picket duty, about the middle of November 1864, and marched up Shoal Creek and joined the balance of our corps. The first town I now recollect of passing thro' was Lawrenceburg, Tennessee, and from there on to Columbia. About the second day's march we were joined by Forrest's Cavalry. They had a few days before taken some Federal transports on the Tennessee River, and many of them had two or three pairs of new shoes tied to their saddles and at first they gave them away to the barefooted infantry until they had only those on their feet, then at night the barefooted infantry stole those they wore; for they said it was no harm for a cavalrymen to be barefooted, as he had a horse to ride. When this expedition started, I think it was intended to forage on the country for supplies to feed the army; and at that time bread was scarce, and the men to get bread would, as soon as camp was struck at night, fell a large tree and cut a square hole in the body of it as deep as it could be cut with a pole axe, and when the chips were cleared out nicely, about a pint of shelled corn put in, and we began to pound it with a pestle, slowly at first, then harder after the grains were cracked, and then sifted out the finest meal; put back the rest and pound again, sift out the meal and then use the coarsest for hominy. We called this going to Armstrong's mill; and it was surprising how soon we could get enough meal for supper, and while supper was cooking we generally prepared enough for breakfast. We also found plenty of Irish potatoes and pumpkins, all which we used. We would buy pork occasionally, and when we could not buy it somebody would go foraging and kill a hog and skin it; but that was dangerous work, for when caught generally a hog-skining cravat was gotten, by taking a piece of hog-skin, cutting a hole in it and slipping it over the offenders head and making him wear it all day with the Provost guard. Some times they would have to carry a fence rail all day in addition to their accoutrements. None of Company K was ever caught or had a hog-skin cravat, or carried a rail, but we got our share of meat all the same." 3

In November 1864, "When the army arrived at Columbia, S.D. Lee's Corps or at least—Johnson's Division, they camped some three or four miles south of town, near the fine farm said to be owned by the Polk's at that time. For two or three days—then we, that is Johnson's Division; were part of the army sent to flank the Federals out of Columbia. We marched east, crossed the Duck River on a pontoon bridge, and again struck the turnpike two or three miles south of Spring Hill; but that day our division was guard for the wagon train and artillery, but I think we had only ordnance along with us. Our brigade did not get up until after day light next morning, although we could hear firing during the evening and night proceeding, and we had to push the wagons and artillery out of the mud, for we had left turnpikes and traveled across country roads, and they resembled our prairie roads in the winter time for mud. After 2 O'clock that night the brigade was halted and stacked arms to rest and waited for all the wagon train to get together, and we were allowed to lie down and sleep. Bob Mayes, Green Westbrook, Jim Thompson and I, lay down on a flat lime rock to keep out of the mud, but we did not sleep long, for it was the coldest bed I have ever had; we got up and moved to the mud like the rest, and then slept very well while we lay there. We started the next morning, November 30th, 1864, and joined our division about an hour by sun, where they had stayed most of the night before, and let all the Federal army pass out on the turnpike in four hundred yards, or less of them. Shortly after joining the division I saw two ladies come into our line marching a Federal prisoner in front of them, with a musket at "shoulder arms," and you could have heard the shout that went up as they passed down the lines with their prisoner, for miles. It was said by the men at the time, if a line of battle had been formed across the turnpike that night, the probabilities were that the entire Federal army and wagon train might have been captured; but of that I can only speak from hearsay, as we did not get there until after daylight next morning." 3

"During the morning we were joined by the other two divisions of our corps, that came from Columbia along the turnpike with the remainder of the wagon train, when we pressed on to Franklin, Tennessee, and arrived in front of the place late that evening. Again Johnson's Division was put in line of battle (and the other divisions of our corps held in reserve) and after dark we were advanced through an old field on the extreme left of our line, next to the Harpeth River, and told to hold our fire until we reached the first line of breast works, as Bate's Division were holding the first line of works and were out of ammunition. We did not find Bate's Division, but instead, when about four steps from the works we received a volley of musketry that made a considerable thinning in our lines, but we raised a shout and went at them with loaded guns and carried the works by storm, except where Manigualt's Brigade was; they ran, and left us exposed on our right to a terrible cross fire down our line that sadly next morning from the dead and wounded on the field. During the fight we ran short of ammunition, but caught a Federal ordnance bearer from the other side of the works and pulled him over to us with a box full of cartridges, about one thousand, when we were again in good shooting fix, and we used it well, to make a noise at least, from the looks of a locust thicket in our front next morning." 3

"Here at Franklin, Company K lost, J.S. Grady, captured; J.B McKinney and G.W. Westbrook, wounded. Here, Lott, of Company F and I, had a shooting match with two Federals across the breast works, and at first it looked as if we were to lose, but they had too much tangle leg in them, and we came off the winners; the distance was about eight feet. Next morning early, while reviewing the fight and making report to headquarters of killed, wounded and missing, Bob Mayes, Company K and Ratliff, Company B, came in from a scouting through Franklin with a side of bacon and box crackers, which were very acceptable to us, as for the last two days we had been on short rations, and while discussing the crackers and bacon, Rafe came in with a supply of biscuits and meat for our mess. We stayed at Franklin all that day, December 1st, 1864 and early next started for Nashville." 3

Official records state, that Federal troops making good their retreat to Franklin, on the Harpeth River, Hood ordered an assault upon the entrenched position November 30, in which Johnson's Division took part after dark. In this terrible night battle in the trenches along the parapets Brantley's Brigade, no stronger than a single regiment, lost 76 killed, 140 wounded, 21 missing. 4

ORDER OF BATTLE CONFEDERATE FORCES			
CENTRAL TENNESSEE CAMPAIGN - BATTLES OF FRANKLIN-NASHVILLE			
NOVEMBER 30,1864 - JANUARY 1,1865			
ARMY OF TENNESSEE - C.S.A.			
Commanding: General John B. Hood			
39,000 Men			
LEE''S CORPS:			
Commanding: Lt.Gen. S. D. Lee			
	(SECOND-Wither's) JOHNSON'S DIVISION:		
	Commanding: Maj.Gen. Edward Johnson		
		1st (Loomis'/Dea's) BRIGADE:	
			(5 Alabama Regts)
		2nd (Chalmer's/Sharp's) BRIGADE:	
			(5 Mississippi Regts)
		3rd (Jone's/Anderson's/Brantley's) BRIGADE:	
		Commanding: Brig.Gen. William F. Brantley	
			Cav Co (Foot)
			24th Mississippi
			27th Mississippi
			29th Mississippi
			30th Mississippi
			34th Mississippi
			Mo Btry
		4th (Manigault's) BRIGADE:	
			(3 Alabama Regts, 2 S.C. Regts)
	STEVENSON'S DIVISION:		
	Commanding: Maj.Gen. Carter L. Stevenson		
		CUMMINGS BRIGADE:	
			(4 Georgia Regts)
		PETTUS BRIGADE:	
			(5 Alabama Regts)
	CLAYTON'S DIVISION:		
	Commanding: Maj.Gen. Henry D. Clayton		
		STOVALL BRIGADE:	

			(5 Georgia Regts)
		GIBSON BRIGADE:	
			(8 Louisiana Regts)
		HOLTZCLAW BRIGADE:	
			(5 Alabama Regts)
STEWART'S CORPS:			
Commanding: Lt.Gen. Alexander P. Stewart			
	LORING'S DIVISION:		
	Commanding: Maj.Gen. William W. Loring		
		FEATHERSTON'S BRIGADE:	
			(6 Mississippi Regts)
		ADAM'S BRIGADE:	
			(6 Mississippi Regts)
		SCOTT'S BRIGADE:	
			(5 Alabama Regts, 1 Louisiana Regt)
	FRENCH'S DIVISION:		
	Commanding: Maj.Gen. Samuel French		
		ECTOR'S BRIGADE:	
			(4 Texas Regts, 2 N.C. Regts)
		COCKRELL'S BRIGADE:	
			(7 Missouri Regts)
		SEAR'S BRIGADE:	
			(5 Mississippi Regts)
	WALTHALL'S DIVISION:		
	Commmanding: Maj.Gen. Edward C. Walthall		
		QUARLES'S BRIGADE:	
			(6 Tennessee Regts, 1 Alabama Regt)
		CANTLEY'S BRIGADE:	
			(3 Alabama Regts, 1 Mississippi Regt)
		REYNOLD'S BRIGADE:	
			(5 Arkansas Regts)
CHEATHAM'S CORPS:			
Commanding: Maj.Gen. Benjamin F. Cheatham			
	CLEBURNE'S DIVISION:		

	Commanding: Maj.Gen. Patrick Celburne		
		(Mercer's) SMITH'S BRIGADE:	
			(4 Georgia Regts)
		4th (Wood) LOWERY BRIGADE:	
			(3 Mississippi Regts, 3 Alabama Regts)
		2nd (Liddell) GOVAN BRIGADE:	
			(10 Arkansas Regts)
		GRANBURY BRIGADE:	
			(8 Texas Regts 1 Tenn Regt, 1 CSA Regt)
	(Cheatham's) BROWN'S DIVISION:		
	Commanding: Maj.Gen. John C. Brown		
		3rd(Maney's) CARTER'S BRIGADE:	
			(5 Tennessee Regts)
		GIST'S BRIGADE:	
			(3 Georgia Regts, 2 S.C. Regts)
		2nd (Stewart)STRAHL'S BRIGADE:	
			(8 Tennessee Regts)
		4th (Smith's/Vaughan's) GORDON'S BRIGADE:	
			(8 Tennessee Regts)
	BATE"S DIVISION:		
	Commanding: Maj.Gen. William B. Bates		
		TYLER's BRIGADE:	
			(4 Tennessee Regts, 1 Georgia Regt)
		3rd (Preston's/Finley's) BRIGADE:	
			(6 Florida Regts)
		JACKSON'S BRIGADE:	
			(4 Georgia Regts, 1 CSA Regt)
CAVALRY CORPS:			
Commanding: Maj.Gen. Nathan B. Forrest			
	CHALMER'S CAV DIVISION:		
	Commanding: Brig.Gen. James R. Chalmers		
		RUCKER'S CAV BRIGADE:	
			(5 Tennessee Regts, 1 Miss Regt, 1 Ala Regt)
		BIFFLE'S CAV BRIGADE:	
			(1 Tennessee Regt)

		BUFORD'S CAV DIVISION:
		Commanding: Brig.Gen. Abraham Buford
		BELL'S CAV BRIGADE:
		(5 Tennesse Regts)
		CROSSLAND'S CAV BRIGADE:
		(5 Kentucky Regts)
		JACKSON'S CAV DIVISION:
		Commanding: Brig.Gen. William H. Jackson
		ARMSTRONG'S CAV BRIGADE:
		(4 Mississippi Regts)
		ROSS'S CAV BRIGADE:
		(3 Texas Regts, 1 Tex Legion)
Re: Bush, Bryan S; The Civil War Battles of the Western Theater; 1998; Pgs 85-87		
Sword, Wiley; Embrace An Angry Wind; The Genl Bks, 1994; Pgs 444-447		

WILLIAMSON COUNTY-FRANKLIN, TENNESSEE, 1864

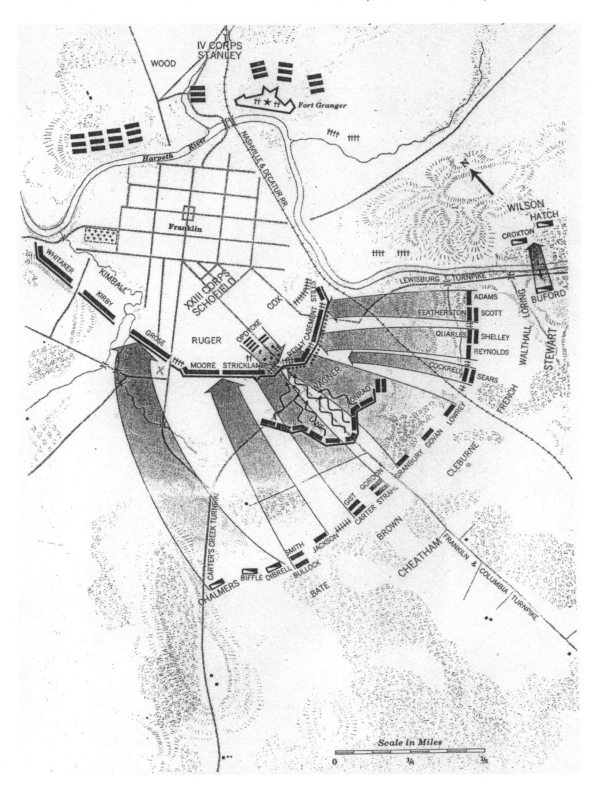

RE: ILLUSTRATED ATLAS OF THE CIVIL WAR

M

PART THREE

THE TWILIGHTS LAST GLEAMING . . .

THE TENNESSEE RETREAT

The Attempted Siege and
Final Battle for Nashville . . .

CHAPTER XI.

NASHVILLE, TENNESSEE: DECEMBER 1864.

"All along the turnpike we found evidence of the hasty retreat made by the Federals, in dead left along the road unburied, and the number of wagons abandoned wherever a team would give out, and frequently, dead mules left to wagons." 3

"That evening we arrived in front of Nashville, and in due course took our position in line of battle, investing Nashville, where we went to work building breast works as if we intended to

Make a regular siege. We prepared our mortars and again begun to pound corn for bread and hominy, and occasionally made a raid on a neighboring hog pen for meat. The men tired of that, so one night four men from the 27th Mississippi borrowed the mules from the tool wagon and visited the supply train, about two miles off, and got three sacks of flour and a side of meat, and the representative of Company K in this raid furnished us with biscuits for several days. Rafe rendered us valuable assistance for foraging for us, but McRae's servant Bob, deserted and went over to the Federals, while Rafe stayed, line of battle except when foraging." 3

"Finally, on December 15th, the Federal commander at Nashville, being heavily reinforced, sallied forth and attacked our lines on the right, and our position being near the center our division was double-quick to support the line where it was attacked. In battle, T.W. Carr, Company K, was captured, and if any were wounded or killed in Company K, do not now recollect it. That day, I had to part company with my old and trusty rifle that I had carried and used so long, for the hammer was blown off; but I soon got another of the same caliber—an imported "Tower" rifle"—that served me well; but it was longer and heavier that the one I had been using." 3

"That night our lines were reformed, and we were this time near the right of the line, and as the battle progressed on December 16th, we were moved to support the extreme right of our lines, and while we lay here in reserve behind a hill, it seems as if the Federals were shooting crooked cannons from the forts and batteries in Nashville, fro' they could throw their shells right in our midst, and from killed and wounded men and horses, a small branch in our rear ran red with blood, that is bloody water." 3

Official records record, "At the battle of Nashville, December 15, Brantley's men, sent to the support of Stewart's Division, endeavored to check the Federal advance on the Granny White pike. Next day, they were moved to the right of Lee's line, where they repulsed a Federal attack, when the line broke on their left and fell back with the army at Brentwood." 4

DAVIDSON COUNTY-NASHVILLE, TENNESSEE 1864

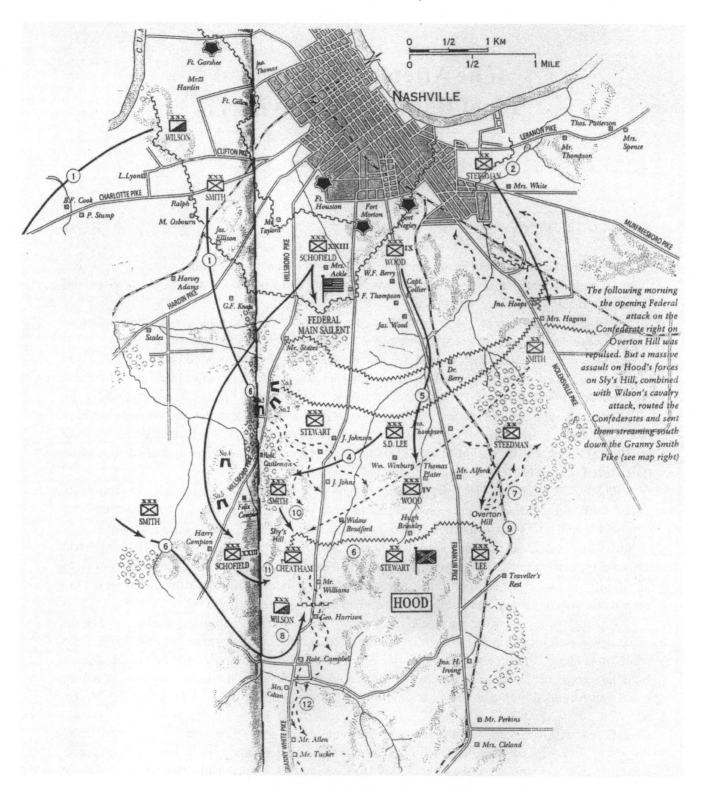

RE: ILLUSTRATED ATLAS OF THE CIVIL WAR

M

The Carolina Campaign—
Retreat and Final Surrender . . .

CHAPTER XII.

BRENTWOOD, TENNESSEE: DECEMBER 1864.
"THE RETURN BACK TO MISSISSIPPI"

Tennessee: "Finally, late in the evening, with but little fighting on our part of the line, our line broke, then stampeded to our left and to the left of the Franklin turnpike, and we were forced to retreat by marching east instead of south, and it finally became dark so we were not pressed hard; but they pressed hard on those that retreated by the turnpike. After dark, Gen. Brantley passed a guide and put him in charge of sick men, with orders to shoot him if he betrayed us to the enemy. He piloted us out safe, and we struck the turnpike five or six miles from Franklin, and in rear of where the Confederates had again formed a line of battle. Up to this time we had no straggling from our brigade, as all feared capture, but when the men found out that a line of battle was between them and enemy, they began to straggle and when stopped south of Franklin, after midnight, there were only four men in the consolidated company to stack arms, and when rations was brought to us we had a full supply, and when Rafe came to us from the cook wagon, we had only four in our mess, as much as we cared to pack with us the next day. Next morning, the stragglers began to come in early, before we got up, for they were hungry. That evening we were camped near Spring Hill, Tennessee, as rear guard, and during the night a squad of Federal Cavalry dashed through our lines, but did no damage that I now remember. We were in the rear until we crossed the Duck River at Columbia. Here at Columbia we rested one day, and during the day it rained very hard. When we left Columbia for Pulaski, we were put with the pontoon train as guard, and ordered to push for the Tennessee River. When we got to Pulaski in the evening, it was sleeting, and next morning the ground was covered with snow several inches deep. We were camped that night on a high hill, with nothing to make fires of except green beach and gum; but we moved rails from a distance of near half a mile to make fires, and when we once got good fires burning we soon got comfortably warm. Some of the regiment that were noted foragers, that night, slept in hen houses in Pulaski with the intention of getting chickens next morning, but the chickens beat them up and they lost their game for that day. We did not go far the next day; only passed Pulaski and crossed the Elk River, a short distance." 3

"Next morning we began the retreat in good earnest. The night before we got back to Shoals Creek a colored driver in the supply train brought to our mess a side of meat and some flour, and wanted his supper. He said he could get supplies, but could not cook it; and it was very acceptable, for that night we had only Irish potatoes for supper; but it was a bad chance to cook flour with nothing to bake it in, so we boiled some meat and potatoes together until about done, when someone suggested that we have what they called at home "drop dumplings," which was make the flour into a batter for flap jacks, and while potatoes and meat were boiling, to drop in a spoonful of batter at a time, and we eventually stirred the whole together, at supper that night, and next morning for breakfast, and cutting it out of the camp kittle, we got meat, bread and potatoes all in the same slice. We arrived at Shoal Creek about the middle of the evening on December 24th, 1864, there was about four inches of snow on the ground, and were ordered to wade the creek. Some rolled up their pants but as soon as the icy waters touched their naked legs they came out of it and no persuasion or coaxing could get the brigade in until General Brantley's horse stepped on a slick rock in the creek and fell him, ducking him good. Then the men took to the water like ducks, laughing as they went. The water was very, very cold; but there was a row of fences, fired for us to warm by on the south bank. After warming a short while we were told for every man to get a piece of fire, as were going into camp for the night, close by." 3

"Next morning we were up and marching for the Tennessee River, where we began at once to put in a pontoon bridge, just below the shoals in the river where there used to be a little town called Bainbridge. The first thing done was to lash two or three pontoon boats together and use them as a ferry boat to cross over some artillery and horses to go towards Florence and protect our bridge from Federal gun boats until the army could cross. We had the bridge completed by 3 O'clock that night, when at once the wagon train started over." 3

Alabama: "While here on the flat on the Tennessee River and the whole army; camped on the bluffs above, it looked like a hard place to forage at; but one of Company K, and three other men of the regiment went foraging; one of the men was barefooted too; that night from cavalry headquarters of General Jackson's they got a pair of boots that fit the barefooted man, a sack of flour about 50 pounds, and a camp kettle of beef off the fire. After the wagon train and most of the infantry had crossed over, our division was crossed over on Tuesday, December 27th, (1864), and as soon as the division was over, I got leave of absence of 24 hours to visit my paternal grandmother who lived about four miles off. I got to grandma's just after dinner, but had a good dinner fixed for me and left next morning, rejoining my command at Cherokee, below Tuscumbia on the Memphis & Charleston railroad after dark that night, when I called for Company K; and Reid of Company F, who had carried my gun and accoutrements for me, poured out the contents of my haver sack, and after supper pulled out several twists of home-made tobacco and then for a smoke by all hands. We continued down the M. & C. railroad to Burnsville, where we crossed over to Rienzi, on the M. & O. railroad. While at Burnsville we were mustered, but I do not know what became of the muster rolls made here, in fact I don't recollect now of writing them. When we got to Rienzi, it was reported that we would go into winter quarters near there, and on the strength of it that morning we sent out scouts for supplies. Adjutant Crump and Capt. Pegg commanding the regiment furnished the horses for some of his Company to ride. The men were gone all day and night and it looked as if we were to have to report them as deserters, but next morning just as we were reporting after the first hours march, the four men came in, much to our relief. The evening before, several men were scouting or rather foraging and furnished us with plenty of pork." 3

"We continued our march south along the M. & C. railroad until we reached Tupelo, Mississippi, were several companies from North Mississippi in the brigade received a furlough for ten days. I also furloughed Rafe and sent him home to get clothing for Company K." 3

Mississippi: "The first night that we were at Tupelo, we camped east of the railroad, but next day we moved west of town and went into camp, where it was said we would go into winter quarters and rest and recruit up. But, Company K was tired and determined not to do any more work than absolutely necessary for comfort. So we split a large poplar log and turned the halves up edge-way and stretched out Yankee dog-tents over it and filled up with leaves to make a bed, and just had a camp fire in front. After we had been thus in camp for five or six days, we all petitioned for a ten day furlough. In a few days there was a general order issued to give ten days furlough to all that could get home in the regiment and brigade, the furlough to be signed only by Brigade commander. I went to work and wrote out Company K, and so dated our furloughs that we got eleven instead of ten days. It was not discovered by Gen. Brantley until he had signed them, when he laughed and said, he would let it go—but to see that no one else caught him." 3

"So late, in the evening of January 19th, 1865, we all left camp with our furloughs dated to begin the next morning, and started home a-foot, as there was no regularity in the trains on the railroad, but all fell out by the time we reached Verona, except J.S. Thompson and I, of Company K, and two of Company A, that were from Oktibbeha county—Sansing and Livingstone. When we got to Okolona, Thompson left us and went across the country home, and here Sansing and Livingstone went a foraging among "butter milk rangers," (home cavalry) that were camped in some old cars close by, and stole enough for our supper. Next morning before day, I started home alone and got there about an hour by sun." 3

Official records show, "The brigade crossed the Tennessee River, December 26, and moved to the vicinity of Tupelo for winter quarters. The brigade was furloughed until February 12, 1865. Under orders for the Carolinas 152 of the brigade assembled at Meridian, February 14." 4

RALEIGH, NORTH CAROLINA: FEBRUARY 1865.
"THE FINAL CAROLINA CAMPAIGN"

"While camped at Tupelo, I lost a diary that was very full, that I had kept of the whole Georgia campaign, and our trip into Tennessee, and if I now had it, it would be very interesting. The next day after we left Tupelo the army began to move to North Carolina, and instead of rendezvousing at Tupelo, we were rendezvousing at Meridian, then the first of February, 1865, and remained there, I think until the 19th of February." 3

Alabama: On February 20th, 1865 "Gen. Sharpe's brigade, was moved to Montgomery, Alabama, where we were encamped out beyond the State House, we were told not to cut any timber in the woods where we were, as it belonged to a crippled Confederate soldier, and that there would be wood hauled for us. At first, the wood was hauled for us, but soon found out that the land did not belong to a crippled soldier, but to a man that had on his gin breast, in large brass letters, "Hon. Bolen Hall;" but we did not think him honorable! For a while we were there, there was a long rainy spell, and it rained very hard, and he would not let the men at night sleep under his gin house, or in it, and the two brigades, when they found him out, and all about him, eat up his market garden. While here in Montgomery, we were mustered, and had to make out muster rolls. Then Lieutenant Welch, of Company L, 27th Mississippi, and myself put on our nicest clothes, blacked our shoes, and went to Mr. Hall's house and ask for the use of a table in his back hall to write on, when we were told that his daughters were at home that day, and to come back next week and he would accommodate us. When told of the urgency of the case, he said his daughters were at home, and shut the door in our face, and then we were forced to go more than a mile, through a hard rain, to Montgomery to do our writing. (And when, after the surrender, we came home and saw that the Federal Cavalry had been there and burned his gin house and cotton bales for him, no one felt sorry.) After this Bob Mayes went to see the Post Quartermaster, Captain Lanier, and he had at one time be wagon master for Capt. Lanier, he loaned us a new wall tent and sent it to us; then Company K, was all comfortably sheltered, as there was only six or seven present. When we left Montgomery, March 9th, 1865, Capt. Lanier sent a dray after the tent, and also got a box containing our overcoats and other heavy winter clothing; promising to send it to us next winter, wherever we might be, free of charge; (but before another winter came, we were at home as quiet citizens, and besides the Federal Cavalry had captured Montgomery and burned the warehouse in which our clothing was stored.) The morning we broke camp at Montgomery it began to rain; and by the time we arrived at the West Point Depot, it was raining nearly in torrents, but we went along with a shout, and finally boarded a train nearly all of us were wet." 3

Georgia: "Our route (by rail) was by Opelika, Alabama, to Macon and Milledgeville, on by way of Sparta, Mayfield to Camak, where we (transferred) to cars for Augusta, (Georgia); where we arrived that evening and marched through the city during a (another) very hard rain, and that night camped across the Savannah River in Hamburg, South Carolina." 3

South Carolina: "Next day, March 17th, (1865) we remained in camp, I and many of the men had the privilege of visiting Augusta. Here we found the prices of everything very high. I recollect of having $300 offered me by a shoemaker for my boots, but he asked me $400 for a pair of shoes, and he actually charged me $30 for pegging my boot in the instep where it had ripped. In pricing some provisions, meal was selling at $60 per bushel; meat $2.50 to $3 per pound; so you see, a Confederate soldier could not by much on $11 per month, and when rations were scarce, it forced them to forage for his supplies. Next day, we left Hamburg, and I cannot tell, from the worn condition of my memoranda, how far we marched, or at what places we went. We crossed the Saluda River, I think, near Ninety-Six (of Revolutionary fame), on the railroad bridge as we went from the river bottom to the hills, where there was an arch of evergreens spanning the road, and the men were invited, if time permitted, (and you know a soldier always had time to get something to eat), to fall out and go to the house near by and get something to eat, for it was the intention at first to hand a snack to every man as he passed, but it was just raining in torrents, Bob Meyers, from Company K, however, fell out and brought us back a full haversack of nice eating's. I would have gone myself, but I was First Sergeant, and had, at the time, command of six companies of the regiment, (for the regiment was divided into two companies, for convenience; among the other five there were two or three commissioned officers, but not one in our six.) We went into camp about three miles from the place above spoken of. Next day, March 22nd, (1865) we marched 19 miles, passed Cross Hill, and encamped. During the day, as we were passing a farm house, and old lady said, "If I had known all you soldiers was to pass here, I would haven given you a dinner, if it had taken a whole hog." Little did she know of the eating qualities of a soldier? On the 23rd we passed Laurens Court House, South Carolina, and the memoranda says we saw 450 ladies, and reckon it was true, for the streets were lined with them passing plates of nice things to the men, (GOD bless them), for they certainly knew a soldier loved to eat, they also gave hats, handkerchiefs, etc.; for we were the first lot of real live soldiers, I expect they ever saw." 3

"March 24th, (1865) we marched 16 miles, passed Mount Shoals, next day marched 16 miles and passed Glenn Springs and Jamesville; Sunday, March 26th, marched to and crossed the Broad River. After we went into camp, near Broad River; Rafe was sent foraging and came back laughing . . . . He had found a good thing for the mess. . . . . Rafe palmed him off as a . . . to the owner of the farm they had gone to. They asked a heap of . . . . Drilled him, and finally satisfied the Negro foreman . . . . As to his identity, when they fixed him up a nice supper, they killed four old hens and baked them, about a . . . . And a quantity of hard boiled eggs. About midnight Bob and I . . . . Laughing, and showing their trophies of that night's foraging." 3

"March 27th, 1865, we left camp on Broad River, at 1 O'clock p.m. and marched 9 miles, and next day marched 14 miles to Chester, South Carolina. While there, we saw what were said to be the lithograph stones (I believe they were called) that were used by the Confederate Government to print the bonds and currency with which to pay the troops, purchase supplies, etc., and from the pile, more than a car load, it seemed as if they might have made it fast enough to keep from being behind with the troops, for we had not been paid to later date than June 3rd, 1864. So you see it must have been patriotism instead of money the poor Confederate fought for." 3

North Carolina: "March 29th, we boarded the cars at Chester, and that day went to Salisbury, North Carolina, next day we traveled all day in the rain to Greensboro, and you can imagine it was anything but pleasant to be crowded in an old box car a day and night and it raining hard most of the time. Today, we passed and had a hand-shaking with part of Company K, that had been prisoners of war at Rock Island for about sixteen months, and were on their way home after being exchanged, and I tell you it felt like meeting your brother who had been long absent, besides we hoped to soon have them back with us, for we were hardly a corporal's guard present for a whole company. But our hand-shaking and talking were short, for both trains were on the move soon, in opposite directions. Next day, March 31st, we passed Raleigh, N.C., and that night camped at Smithfield, North Carolina, and this was another day of constant rain." 3

"While our train was at Raleigh, we took aboard with us a few Mississippi troops that had been cut off from their command at the battle of Bentonville, about two days before, and had just made their way back to Raleigh. While we were stopped at Raleigh, I went out to hunt something to eat for the mess, and made out to buy three biscuits at one dollar each. That night in Smithfield, I got on the good side of the Sergeant of the Guard, who was guarding the box that had our commissary stores in it, and got a shoulder and side of bacon, and a peck of meal, and then be came and ate supper with us about eleven O'clock at night. The meal was so small that shoulder and side were cut together and both did not weight over ten or twelve pounds and we ate the most of it that night, for we had been on the cars and on short rations for the past three days, with no chance to forage." 3

"April 1st, we marched to Smithfield and rejoined our division, after an absence of two months. Two days later, on April 4th, 1865 it says "grand review of the Army of Tennessee," but does not say who by, but I suppose by General Johnston, Beauregard and Hood.

For the next few days nothing of interest transpired only daily drill, morning and evening. It put duty pretty hard on me as Orderly Sergeant, to make reports for six companies, and attend to all other duties as First Sergeant, and then to have to act as drill master, for as yet we had no commissioned officers among us. April 10th, we broke camp and marched out when there was a general reorganization of the army. The 24th, 27th, 29th, 30th and 34th Mississippi regiments were organized into one regiment, to be known as the 24th Mississippi regiment. Company K, and others to number of about four, were known as Company F, commanded by Capt. Wilson (of the old 34th). I do not remember the First Lieutenant; I was promoted to Second Lieutenant. Capt. Jack Evans, with two Mississippi companies from an Alabama regiment, was Company A, in the new organization. Capt. Williamson, of the 29th Mississippi, was made Colonel, for some reason, I do not now remember, he was generally called by the men "Old Step High." Capt. Dancey, of the 24th was made Lieutenant-Colonel, and he was a very nice and pleasant gentleman; previous to this, he had been with Gen. Brantley (now dead) was known to the brigade as "Bull of the Woods." I think Gen. Dea's commanded the division, consisting of Brantley's and Sharpe's brigades. After the reorganization it was said we would go into camp again where we were, but less than an hour the bugle sounded, and in a short time we were put in motion towards Raleigh, where we arrived the next day. The next day, I think it was the 12th of April, we heard Gen. Lee had surrendered to Gen. Grant. We continued our march back to Greensboro, where we arrived on April 16th, and went into camp at and around the Court House, and here on the doors we saw an official notice of the surrender of Gen. Lee. We were here put on guard over all public property, both Confederate and state of North Carolina, and to keep down all rioting and disorder of every character. We kept the streets around the different supply depots guarded day and night, permitting no one, unless with a pass, to come in. I even saw what was said to be the gold and silver, in boxes and kegs, loaded in wagons, under strong cavalry guard, started south. We here received $1.15 per man in silver, and later on some received more. I here got a good pair of what was called English army shoes and enough Confederate grey cloth to make a suit of clothes when I got home. Some went nearly every night to headquarters and ask the General's Johnston and Beauregard what would be done. April 21st, General Walthall and Governor Vance made speeches to us. On the 27th of April (Official records indicate April 26, 1865) we were notified that we had been surrendered to the Federal army, and two days later we stacked our arms around the Court House at Greensboro, and marched out and gave possession to the Federal advance guard. While here it was necessary to keep a strong guard at the government stock yard to prevent the mules and horses from being stolen, there was a detail of 20 men from our regiment for the purpose, and Bob Mayes, of old Company K, was among the number." 3 1

The Trip home: "We left Greensboro; each one of them was given a horse or mule to ride home. Boy Mayes called his horse "Abe Lincoln," and when rested up he was a very good horse. Here at Greensboro there was a large map of the United States hanging on the wall of the Court House, and I daresay, it was consulted oftener while we were there a few days than it had been in as many years before; the men with strings and straws trying to compute or measure the distance to be traveled to reach their respective homes again. After April 30th, 1865, I know that we marched together as a command, with roll call and all, until we reached the railroad from Columbia to Abbeville, South Carolina, where all Company K called for their paroles, and took cars to Abbeville, then walked across to Washington, Georgia; then by cars to Atlanta, and on to West Point, Georgia; then marched to Montgomery, Alabama as the railroad had been destroyed by Federal Cavalry. Twenty-five miles from Montgomery, I was taken sick and had to lay over for two days, and all of the company left me, except Rafe, and when I got to Montgomery, I found all had passed thro' and had gone home except Frank Evans, and he had left me, I left him here to get home as best he could, and have never seen him since. All the rest of Company K that were present I have often seen, and besides all those nearly that I now know to be living. 3

The Official record details the progress of the brigade eastward. "They started east on the 18th and were detained some time at Montgomery by the Mobile campaign. In March, they proceeded to Augusta and thence to North Carolina. April 3, the aggregate present to the brigade was 283 (men)". The new consolidated 24th regiment with the 2nd Alabama, and 58th N.C., representing consolidated fragments of other brigades, constituted the brigade of General W. F. Brantley, in D. H. Hill's Division of S. D. Lee's Corps. The Army surrendered April 26, and paroled at Greensboro, N.C., soon afterward." 4 2

Post Script: Unbeknown to the men of the old 27th Mississippi regiment, their first commander, Colonel T. M. Jones, was not very far away from the regiment in March 1865; as he was in command of Fort Caswell and the 1st N.C. (Arty) Battalion, on the North Carolina coast. Gen. Schofield's attacks on the coastal fortification, forced withdrawal from all coastal fortifications, including Fort Caswell; this required the 1st N.C. Battalion to join with Hagood's brigade, which fought a delaying action at Town Creek, on March 7th, and later fought at the Battle of Bentonville, before being surrendered! 5

ORDER OF BATTLE CONFEDERATE FORCES		
CAROLINA'S CAMPAIGN - BATTLE OF BENTONVILLE		
MARCH 19-20, 1865		
CONFEDERATE FORCES: General Joseph E. Johnston		
ARMY OF TENNESSEE - C.S.A.		
Commanding: Lt.Gen. Alexander P. Stewart		
15,000 Men　　　(Surrendered: 89,000 Men)		
CHEATHAM'S CORPS:		
Commanding:		
	CLEBURNE'S DIVISION:	
		Smith's Brigade:(Georgia)
		Lowery's Brigade: (Alabama)
		Govan's Brigade: (Arkansas)
		Granbury's Brigade: (Texas)
	BATE"S DIVISION:	
		Tyler's Brigade: (Georgia)
		Finley's Brigade: (Florida)
	BROWN'S DIVISION:	
		Gist's Brigade: (Georgia)
		Maney's Brigade: (Tennessee)
		Strahl's Brigade: (Tennessee)
		Vaughan's Brigade: (Tennessee)
LEE'S CORPS:		
Commanding:		
	STEVESON'S DIVISION:	
		Cumming's Brigade: (Georgia)
		Pettus's Brigade: (Alabama)
		Palmer's Brigade: (Confederate)
	HILL'S DIVISION:	
		Dea's Brigade: (Alabama)
		Manigault's Brigade: (South Carolina)
	CLAYTON'S DIVISION:	

		Stovall's Brigade: (Georgia)
		Baker's Brigade: (Alabama)
		Jackson's Brigade: (Georgia)
STEWART'S CORPS:		
Commanding:		
	LORING'S DIVISION:	
		Featherston's Brigade: (Mississippi)
		Lowery's Brigade: (Mississippi)
		Scott's Brigade: (Alabama)
	WALTHALL'S DIVISION:	
		Quarles's Brigade: (Tennessee)
		Reynold's Brigade: (Arkansas)
DEPARTMENT OF NORTH CAROILNA:		
Commanding: General Braxton Bragg		
	HOKE'S DIVISION:	
		Clingman's Brigade: (North Carolina)
		Colquitt's Brigade: (Georgia)
		Hagood's Brigade: (North Carolina)
		Kirkland's Brigade: (North Carolina)
		1st Jr.Res. Brigade: (North Carolina)
		Artillery Brigade: (North Carolina)
		Jackson's Brigade: (North Carolina)
DEPARTMENT OF S.C., GEORGIA, FLORIDA:		
Commanding: Lt.Gen. William J. Hardee		
	MC LAW'S DIVISION:	
		Conner's Brigade: (South Carolina)
		Harrison's Brigade: (Georgia)
		Fiser's Brigade: (Georgia)
		Hardy's Brigade: (North Carolina)
		Blanchard's Brigade: (South Carolina)
	TALIAFERRO'S DIVISION:	
		Rhett's Brigade: (South Carolina)
		Elliott's Brigade: (Georgia)
CAVALRY CORPS:		

Commanding: Lt.Gen. Wade Hampton			
	BUTLER'S DIVISION:		
		Butler's Brigade: (South Carolina)	
		Young's Brigade: (Georgia)	
		Horse Artillery:	
CAVALRY CORPS:			
Commanding: Maj.Gen. Joseph Wheeler			
	HUME'S DIVISION:		
		Ashby's Brigade: (Tennessee)	
		Harrison's Brigade: (Confederate)	
	DIBRELL'S DIVISION:		
		Dibrell's Brigade: (Tennessee)	
		Lewis Brigade: (Kentucky)	
	ALLEN'S DIVISION:		
		Anderson's Brigade: (Confederate)	
		Hagan's Brigade: (Alabama)	
NORTH CAROLINA (OTHER):			
	AOT Scatered units not at Bentonville:		
	BRANTLEY'S BRIGADE: (10 Apr '65)		
	(Assigned Dea's Division, Lee's Corps)		
	Commanding: Col. (Unknown)		
		24th Mississippi Regt.	
		Commanding: Col. Williamson	
			Consolidated:
			24th, 27th, 29th, 30th, 34th Miss
Re: Hughes Jr., Nathanie C., Bentonvill, UNC Presee, Chapel Hill, NC 1996, Appx 1.			
Bush, Bryan S., The Civil War Battles of the Western Theater. 1998. Pg 92.			

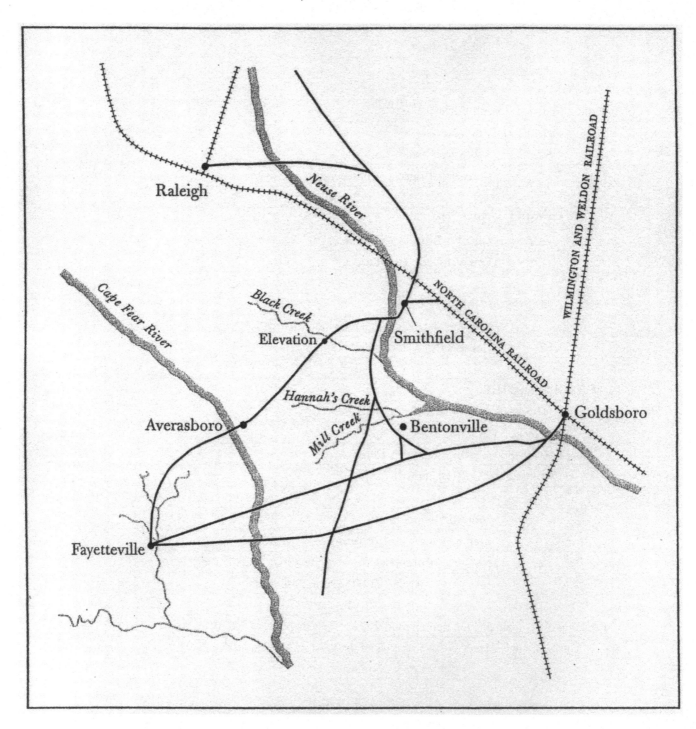

RE: BENTONVILLE

M

TABLE-8

ORDER OF BATTLE CONFEDERATE FORCES
CAROLINA'S CAMPAIGN—FINAL REORGANIZATION
APRIL 10, 1865

CONFEDERATE FORCES: General Joseph E. Johnson
ARMY OF TENNESSEE-C.S.A.

22,000 Men (Western Theater inclusive)

S.D. LEE'S CORPS:
Commanding: Lieutenant-General Stephen D. Lee

   D.H. HILL'S DIVISION
   Commanding:

        BRANTLEY'S BRIGAE:
        Commanding:

             24th Mississippi Infantry Regt.:
             Commanding: COL Williamson (29th)
                           LT-COL Dancey (24th)

                  A / B / C Company (Cons):
                  Commanding: CAPT Wilson (34th)
                                2nd LT Jarman (27th)

             2nd Alabama Infantry Regt.:
             Commanding:

             58th North Carolina Infrantry Regt.:
             Commanding:

        SHARP'S BRIGADE (-):
        Commanding:

        DEA'S BRIGADE (-):
        Commanding:

        MANIGUALT'S BRIGADE (-):
        Commanding: Re: 2, 4

Regimental Casualties 1861-1865 . . .

CHAPTER XIII.

27th Mississippi Regimental Casualties: 1861-1865

(Narrative Battlefield Estimates and Reports)

BATTLES	Killed	Wounded	Missing	POWs
Perryville:	10	40*	?	40*
Murfreesboro:	11	71*	2*	?*
Chickamauga:	10	88*	19*	5?*
Chattanooga:	20	188*	1,666*	8?*
Atlanta:	24	125*	*?	2?*
Franklin:	76	140*	21*	1?*
Nashville:	151	614*	1,708*	57?*
(Raleigh:			101	)

Total Present at Surrendered: 50

Keynotes unknown numbers—?

Keynotes greatest source of POW's—*

Re: Summary of combined sources 3 & 4

Regimental Prisoners-of-War 1862-1865 . . .

CHAPTER XIV.

Regimental (Company K) Prisoners-of-War 1865: 3

Carolina 1865 Campaign:
Montgomery Muster
(Partial return, Company K only) 18

"Listed below as P.O.W.'s"

Officers: 2ⁿᵈ Lt. W.A. Mc Millian
NCO's: 4ᵗʰ Sgt. J.W. Marshall
5ᵗʰ Sgt. T.D. Williamson

Privates: Booth, B.H.
Carr, T.W.,
Cheek, J.H.,
Fears, J.M.,
Gibson, B.F.,
Gladney, J.S.,
Hill, R.E.,
Nash, W.M.,
Peters, R.H.,
Puckett, A.C.,
Porter, T.S.,
Smith, J.M.,
Thrailkill, J.,
Whalley, J.,
Whalley, W.Jr.

The Regimental Tribute-Home Coming . . .

CHAPTER XV.

The Regimental (Company) Tribute and Home Coming.

THIS REPRESENTS THE FINAL MUSTER ROLL OF COMPANY K
(the only know surviving record of the 27th Mississippi Infantry Regiment). 3

"The last Muster Roll of Company K (also earlier known as the Company B, Fifth Battalion Mississippi Infantry), Twenty-Seventh Mississippi Infantry, at Montgomery, Alabama on February 28th, 1865, as follows:

Officers: 2nd Lt. W.A. Mc Millian,	**Prisoner-of-War**
NCOES: 1st Sgt. R.A. Jarman,	**Present for duty**
4th Sgt. J.W. Marshall,	**Prisoner-of-War**
5th Sgt. T.D. Williamson,	**Prisoner-of-War**
Privates: Carroll, J.P.,	**Present for duty**
Evans, F.M.,	"
Mayes, R.L.,	"
McRae, J.S.,	"
Thompson, J.S.	"
Cox, R.J.,	**Detached Service (elsewhere)**
Warner, G.O.	"
Moore, A.W.,	"
Bonner, T.A.,	**Sick or in Hospital**
Colley, J.S.L.,	"
Dean, J.H.,	"
Gideon, J.A.S.,	"
Jones, R.C.,	"
McKinney, J.B.,	"
Savage, Z.T.,	"
Smith, J.E.,	"
Westbrook, W.G.,	"
White, H.V.	"
Booth, B.H., Prisoners-of-War (known to be alive)	

Carr, T.W.,	"
Cheek, J.H.,	"
Fears, J.M.,	"
Gibson, B.F.,	"
Gladney, J.S.,	"
Hill, R.E.,	"
Nash, W.M.,	"
Peters, R.H.,	"
Puckett, A.C.,	"
Porter, T.S.,	"
Smith, J.M.,	"
Thrailkill, J.,	"
Whalley, J.,	"
Whalley, W.Jr.	"

While encamped at Smithfield, North Carolina on 9 April 1865, five Mississippi regiments were ordered to be consolidated (24th, 27th, 29th, 30th and 34th Infantry Regiments) and be redesignated officially as the Twenty-Fourth Mississippi Infantry regiment. 3

The following Officer and Men of the old Company K/27th Mississippi Infantry were surrendered on 27 April 1865 at Raleigh, North Carolina; on the 29 April, the unit ordered to Greensboro, North Carolina to protect State Property. Upon relief, the unit marched in formation to received official paroles at Abbeville, South Carolina on 30 April 1865. 3

(On March 30th, 1865 while transiting Greensboro, N.C. northbound train, made contact with a southbound train carrying approximately 15 men recently paroled Prisoners-of-War, now veterans of Company K/27th Mississippi Infantry heading home for rehabilitation).

May 1st, 1865, all parolees boarded a train enroute to Atlanta, West Point, Montgomery, and onward to their Mississippi homes and families: 3 (Note: General Richard Taylor surrended all Confederate forces in Mississippi-Alabama in late May 1865; with General Kirby Smith, ending the war with the surrendered of his forces in Texas-Louisiana in June 1865)

"Survivors"

Officer: 2nd Lieutenant Jarman, Robert A.
(Elected 10 April '65)
(Formerly Orderly-1st Sergeant/Drillmaster)
(Note: became sick in route)
Accompanied by his personal servant: "Rafe" (Radford Hooks)

Home destination: Aberdeen, Mississippi

Privates: Carroll, Jesse
Evans, Frank (Note: Became sick in route)

Mayes, Bob
McRae, Bob
Thompson, James

Home destination: Monroe Country, Mississippi

Total Surviving Officers and men: 6

*   *   *

H O M E AT LAST!

The Home Coming: "The surviving members of Company K, 27th Mississippi Regiment, were requested to meet at W. A. McMillan & Son's, Saturday, May 3rd, 1890, at 12 O'clock p.m. to take some steps to have a re-union of the Company in July, 1890." 3

Regimental Biographical Sketches . . .

CHAPTER XVI.

The First Regimental Commander
COLONEL Thomas Marshall Jones, PACS.

Thomas Marshall Jones was a native of Virginia born in 1833. He graduated from West Point Military Academy in the class 1853, entering the army as a second lieutenant. Serving various assignments in the regular army through the Seminole Wars of 1837-1841, and later the Mexican-American War of 1846-1848. He resigned as a first lieutenant upon Virginia's secession, and tendered his services to the Confederacy and President Jefferson Davis. He accepted a commission in the rank of Major of the Confederate States Army. In December 1861, his name came highly recommended for a new regimental command from General Cooper with concurrence from President Davis to General Bragg. On January 14, 1862, he was given command of the Twenty-Seventh Mississippi Infantry and promoted to Colonel, PACS. For the next three years his military fortunes would decline, perhaps to internal politics or a general lack of ability in higher command. Initially, the regiment performed well and he was given also command of Pensacola Station, preparing for the successful evacuation on 10 May 1862. Upon rejoining the Army of Tennessee on 18 August 1862, he was given acting command of Anderson's Division during the early stages of the Kentucky Campaign. His success, lead to his commanding the 4th (Mississippi) Brigade during the Battle of Perryville in October 1862. Again, he was trusted to higher command, as acting commander of Walthall's Brigade at the Battle of Murfreesboro on 31 December 1862 were he was wounded and hospitalized. In was reported that he resigned in 1863 (but not record found). There is a service gap, but in January 1865 he reappears as the Post Commander of Fort Caswell, North Carolina and commanding the First North Carolina Artillery Battalion. On 31 March 1865 Fort Caswell is ordered abandoned, with orders to join Brigadier-General Hagood's Brigade of Hoke's Division. Major-General Hoke made a stand at Town Creek, N.C. as a delaying action on 7 March 1865 to slow down union forces. Hoke' Division as a part of the North Carolina Department forces under the command of General Bragg, and joined with General Johnston in the Battle of Bentonville, N.C. on 19-20 March 1865. General Johnston's forces retreated and finally surrendered all personnel on 20 April 1865. Colonel Jones out lived his many peers, passing away in 1903. 1, 4, 5

The First Regimental Sergeant-Major
SERGEANT-MAJOR John P. Carter

John P. Carter a native of Augusta, Mississippi. Mustered with the "Kennedy Guard" on 17 August 1861 at August, Perry County, Mississippi by Captain Julius Kennedy for a period of three years. Initially serving as First Sergeant during the company's training at Camp Brookhaven. Mississippi from August to December 1861. Upon completing training and local recruiting, the Kennedy Guards were ordered to Mobile. Alabama. In January 1862 the company was assigned to the Twenty-Seventh Mississippi Regiment, and designed Company G. He was appointed the Regimental Sergeant-Major, serving through the Battles of Perryville, and following the Battle of Murfreesboro, he was elected a second lieutenant in Company G, on 12 February 1863. He was succeeded as Sergeant-Major by Isom Watkins. At the Battle of Lookout Mountain on 24 November 1863, 2nd Lieutenant Carter was captured and become a prisoner-of-war and imprisoned in Louisville, Kentucky until the end of the war. After the war he returned to Augusta, Mississippi and was active as a Confederate veteran from the 1890's until his passing. 1

NATIONAL ARCHIVES MICROFILM PUBLICATIONS

Microcopy No. 269

COMPILED SERVICE RECORDS OF
CONFEDERATE SOLDIERS WHO SERVED IN
ORGANIZATIONS FROM THE STATE OF
MISSISSIPPI

Roll 326

Twenty-seventh Infantry, A – Ca

THE NATIONAL ARCHIVES
NATIONAL ARCHIVES AND RECORDS SERVICE
GENERAL SERVICES ADMINISTRATION

Washington: 1959

CAPTIONS
AND RECORD OF EVENTS.

(Field and Staff.)

27 MISSISSIPPI INFANTRY.

(Confederate.)

CARD NUMBERS

1	20
2	21
3	22
4	23
5	24
6	25
7	26
8	27
9	28
10	29
11	30
12	31
13	32
14	33
15	34
16	35
17	36
18	37
19	38

Jones Thomas M.

Co. F. S., 27 Mississippi Inf.

(Confederate,)

Colonel   Colonel

CARD NUMBERS

1		20	
2		21	
3		22	
4		23	
5		24	
6		25	
7		26	
8		27	
9		28	
10		29	
11		30	
12		31	
13		32	
14		33	
15		34	
16		35	
17		36	
18		37	
19		38	

Number of medical cards herein

Number of personal papers herein

Book Mark:

See also

(Confederate.)

27   Miss.

T. M. Jones

Col. , 27 Regiment Mississippi Volunteers.

Appears on

Field and Staff Muster Roll

of the organization named above.

for June 30 to Oct. 31   1862

Date of Commission, or } Jan 14 , 1862
Regimental Appointment. }

Station

Present or absent   Present

Remarks: Detached - comdg. H

Brig. 2 Div. Left Wing L. M.

About April 9, 1865, this regiment was consolidated with the 27th, 29th, 30th and 34th Regiments Mississippi Infantry and formed a new regiment which was designated the 24th Regiment Mississippi Infantry.

Book mark:

(849)   Copyist.

C. | 27 | Miss.

J. T. Carter

2d Lieut, Co. G, 27 Reg't Mississippi Inf.

Appears on

Company Muster Roll

of the organization named above,

for Jan & Feb, 186 3.

Enlisted:
When Sept 17, 186 1.
Where Augusta, Miss.
By whom Capt Kennedy
Period 3 yrs or war

Last paid:
By whom Lieut Simmons
To what time Dec 31, 186 2

Present or absent Present

Remarks: Sergt. Maj. 27"
Miss. Regt. was elected
2d Lieut Feb 12, 1863

About April 9, 1865, this regiment was consolidated with
the 24th, 29th, 30th and 34th Regiments Mississippi Infantry,
and formed a new regiment which was designated the 24th
Regiment Mississippi Infantry.

Book mark:

A.W. Parks

Copyist

27 Mis Infantry

Field & Staff

Jones, Thos. M. .... Col

Autry, James .... Lt Col

Hays, A. J. .... 14 Col

Lipscomb, Jno H. .... Maj

Campbell, James A. .... Lt Col

Jones, A. J. .... Adj

McLemore, A. .... Maj

Divine, K. C. .... Surg

Bolan, M. .... Surg

Shelby, J. A. .... A.S.

Buckner, J. W. .... A.S.

Venable, R. I. .... A.S.

Boyle, Jno. M. .... A.C.S.

Jones, Jesse S. .... A.C.S.

Craft, Athson .... A.Q.M.

Williams, C. H. .... A. Litt

Crump, W. .... Sgt

Glasgow, J. M. .... Q.S.K. Apr 2 63

APPENDICIES

Register of Commissioned Officers and Non-Commissioned Officers, Twenty-Seventh Regiment Mississippi Volunteers
(Roster 1)

LAST NAME	FIRST NAME	MI	RANK	POSITION	Footnotes	Page	Ref: 4
Jones	Thomas	M.	Brigadier-General	Commander	Transferred	May1863	
Campbell	James	A.	Colonel	Commander	POW		
Autry	James	L.	Lieutenant-Colonel	Executive Officer	Killed		
Hays	A.	J.	Lieutenant-Colonel	Executive Officer	Transferred	AOT Staff	
Jones	Andrew	J.	Lieutenant-Colonel	Executive Officer	Killed		
Lipscomb	George	H.	Major		Killed		
McLemore	Amos		Major		Killed		
Kennedy	Julius	B.	Major		Killed		
Crump	W.	S.	Staff	Adjutant			
Rice	G.	W.	Staff (2d Lieut.)	Adjutant			
Shelby	Isaac		Staff	Surgeon			
Bolan	W.	J.	Staff	Surgeon			
Divine	K.	C.	Staff	Surgeon	Transferred		
Buckner	J.	S.	Staff	Asst Surgeon			
Shelby	J.	A.	Staff	Asst Surgeon			
Veneable	K.	N.	Staff	Asst Surgeon			
Craft	Addison		Staff	Quartermaster	Transferred		
Denham	G.	B.	Staff (1st Lieut.)	Quartermaster			
Catchings			Lieutenant	Quartermaster			
Williams	C.	H.	Staff	Asst Quartermaster			
Boyles	John		Staff (2d Lieut.)	A. Commiss. Sub.			
Jones	Jesse	S.	Staff	A. Commiss. Sub.			
Grayson	J.	W.	Staff	A. Commiss. Sub.			
Gladney	S.	M.	Staff	A.S.K.			
Carter	J.	P.	Sergeant-Major	HQs	POW	2d Lieut.	
Watkins	Isom		Sergeant-Major	HQs			

OKTIBBEHA COUNTY							
COMPANY - A	Starksville, MS	MS	Oktibbeha Rifles	Infantry	8 Jun 1861		
Huntley	E.	O.	Captain	Co Commander	Killed		
Huntley	M.	C.	First-Lieutenant	Co Officer	Died		
Hannah	William	M.	First-Lieutenant	Co Officer			
Adams	N.	Q.	Second-Lieutenant	Co Officer			
Hannah	T.	L.	Second-Lieutenant	Co Officer			
Fowler	John		Second-Lieutenant	Co Officer	Killed		
Hendon	W.	L.	Second-Lieutenant	Co Officer			

JONES COUNTY							
COMPANY - B	Ellisville	MS	Rosin Heels	Infantry	10 Aug 1861		
McLemore	Amos	M.	Captain	Co Commander	Killed		
Pegg	Samuel	M.	Captain	Co Commander			
Welborn	Joel	E.	First-Lieutenant	Co Officer	Transferred		
Smith	Siman	H.	First-Lieutenant	Co Officer			
Cooper	Norman		First-Lieutenant	Co Officer			
Bayliss	J.	M.	Second-Lieutenant	Co Officer	Transferred		
Grayson	John	W.	Second-Lieutenant	Co Officer	*		
Grayson	G.	W.	Second-Lieutenant	Co Officer			

LINCOLN COUNTY							
COMPANY - C	Brookhaven	MS	Fredonia Hards	Infantry	6 Sep 1861		
Jones	Andrew	J.	Captain	Co Commander	Killed	Major	
Poole	John	R.	Captain	Co Commander	Killed		
Tardy	B.	A.	First-Lieutenant	Co Officer	Died		
Wiley	W.	W.	First-Lieutenant	Co Officer	Disabled		
Major	J.	M.	Second-Lieutenant	Co Officer			
King	J.	R.	Second-Lieutenant	Co Officer	Resigned		
Smith	George	T.	Third-Lieutenant	Co Officer	Died		
Rivers	Elisha	F.	Third-Lieutenant	Co Officer			
Switzer	D.	S.	Third-Lieutenant	Co Officer			

LINCOLN COUNTY							
COMPANY - D	**Brookhaven**	**MS**	**Rayburn Rifles**	**Infantry**	**28 Aug 1861**		
Nielson	E.	R.	Captain	Co Commander	Killed		
Hall	William	W.	Captain	Co Commander	Transferred		
Brown	Philander	P.	Captain	Co Commander			
Bailey	Thomas	S.	First-Lieutenant	Co Officer			
Brown	James	H.	Second-Lieutenant	Co Officer	Killed		
Noel	John	E.	Second-Lieutenant	Co Officer			
Rice	George	W.	Second-Lieutenant	Co Officer			

LEAKE COUNTY							
COMPANY - E	**Carthage**	**MS**	**Leake Guards**	**Infantry**	**25 Apr 1861**		
Campbell	James	A.	Captain	Co Commander	Killed	Major	
Boyd	John	S.	Captain	Co Commander			
Drake	Jabez		First-Lieutenant	Co Officer			
Edwards	M.	C.	First-Lieutenant	Co Officer	Killed		
Edwards	J.	M.	First-Lieutenant	Co Officer			
Colbert	W.	B.	First-Lieutenant	Co Officer			
Allen	M.		First-Lieutenant	Co Officer			
McIntosh	Samuel		Second-Lieutenant	Co Officer	Resigned		
Parrott	A.	J.	Second-Lieutenant	Co Officer	Dropped		
Harper	W.	T.	Second-Lieutenant	Co Officer			
Ward	W.	E.	Second-Lieutenant	Co Officer	Resigned		
Hull	R.	J.	Second-Lieutenant	Co Officer			
Nash	J.	M.	Third-Lieutenant	Co Officer			

COVINGTON COUNTY							
COMPANY - F	**Williamsburg, MS**	**MS**	**Covington Fencibles**	**Infantry**	**3 May 1861**		
McLaurin	Hugh	R.	Captain	Co Commander	Died		
Baugh	Joel	R.	Captain	Co Commander			
Eaton	William	J.	First-Lieutenant	Co Officer			
McLeod	D.	J.	First-Lieutenant	Co Officer	Killed		

McLeod	Daniel	A.	Second-Lieutenant	Co Officer			
Gist	Samuel	H.	Second-Lieutenant	Co Officer			
Lott	W.	J.	Second-Lieutenant	Co Officer	Killed		
Gill	S.	H.	Second-Lieutenant	Co Officer			
Applewhite	W.	L.	Second-Lieutenant	Co Officer	Killed		

PERRY COUNTY							
COMPANY - G	**August**	**MS**	**Kennedy Guards**	**Infantry**	**17 Sept 1861**		
Kennedy	Julius	B.	Captain	Co Commander	Killed	Major	
Byrd	John	S.	Captain	Co Commander			
Denham	George	B.	First-Lieutenant	Co Officer			
Booth	William	P.	Second-Lieutenant	Co Officer			
Carter	John	P.	Second-Lieutenant	Co Officer	Commiss.	(Sgt-Maj*)	
Thompson	John	M.	Second-Lieutenant	Co Officer			
Campbell	S.	A.	Second-Lieutenant	Co Officer	Resigned		
JASPER COUNTY							
COMPANY - H	**Paulding**	**MS**	**Jasper Blues**	**Infantry**	**1 Aug 1861**		
Nixon	Goodwin		Captain	Co Commander	Resigned		
Stafford	E.	W.	Captain	Co Commander			
Brame	W.	M.	First-Lieutenant	Co Officer			
Rogers	Michael		First-Lieutenant	Co Officer			
Phillips	J.	T.	Second-Lieutenant	Co Officer	Resigned		
Morris	B.	F.	Second-Lieutenant	Co Officer			
McCormick	James	U.	Second-Lieutenant	Co Officer	Resigned		
Bufkin	J.	L.	Second-Lieutenant	Co Officer			
Terrel	James		Third-Lieutenant	Co Officer	Resigned		

JASPER COUNTY							
COMPANY - I	**Paulding**	**MS**	**Harris Rebels**	**Infantry**	**20Sept1861**		
Harris	A.	J.	Captain	Co Commander	Resigned		
Wood	John	H.	Captain	Co Commander	Killed		
Jones	Alexander		First-Lieutenant	Co Officer			

Kilgore	Alfred		First-Lieutenant	Co Officer			
Madden	J.	C.	Second-Lieutenant	Co Officer			
Burrus	J.	C.	Third-Lieutenant	Co Officer	Killed		
Hyde	J.	J.	Third-Lieutenant	Co Officer	Resigned		
Thompson			Third-Lieutenant	Co Officer			

MONROE COUNTY							
COMPANY - K	Aberdeen	MS	Enfield Rifles	Infantry	27 Sept 1861 Paroled 28 Feb 1985: Montgomery, Ala		
Sales	John	B.	Captain	Co Commander	Transferred	&	
Saunders	W.	H.	Captain	Co Commander		&	
Snowden	A.	V.	Captain	Co Commander	Killed	&	
Evans	William	B.	First-Lieutenant	Co Officer		&	
McMillan	W.	A.	Second-Lieutenant	Co Officer		POW	
Kelsh	W.	A.	Second-Lieutenant	Co Officer	Resigned		
Powell	Andrew	G.	Second-Lieutenant	Co Officer		&	
Powell	Anderson	G.	Second-Lieutenant	Co Officer	Died	&	
Jarman	Jonathan	J.	Second-Lieutenant	Co Officer	Died	&	
Jarman	R.	A.	Orderly-Sergeant			P	

COMPANY - L	Pascaguola	MS	Twiggs Rifles	Infantry	20 Oct 1861		
Griffin	H.	B.	Captain	Co Commander			
Hawkins	T.	R.	First-Lieutenant	Co Officer			
Johnson	S.	M.	First-Lieutenant	Co Officer	Wounded		
Welch	William		First-Lieutenant	Co Officer			
Thompson	J.	G.	Second-Lieutenant	Co Officer	Died		
McInnis	J.	M.	Second-Lieutenant	Co Officer			
Krebs	H.	E.	Third-Lieutenant	Co Officer			
Baptiste	Antonio		First-Sergeant		Killed		

Complete Regimental Muster Roster of Officers and Men serving from 1861 thru 1865

PERSONNEL INDEX NAME-TWENTY SEVENTH MISSISSIPPI INFANTRY REGIMENT, VOLUNTEERS

ROSTER-2

27th Regimental Field & Staff: Pensacola, FL   14Jan1862 to   1May1865

27th Regiment, Mississippi Infantry				
First Name	Last Name	Company	Rank_In	Rank_Out
Cornelius	Adams	A	Private	Private
Non Q.	Adams	A	Private	Second Lieutenant
James	Akewman	I	Private	Private
A. T.	Alexander	C	Private	Private
Allen F.	Alexander	C	Private	Private
John B.	Alexander	L	Private	Private
John R.	Alexander	L	Private	Private
George P.	Alhered	P	Private	Private
Benjamin F.	Allbritton	A	Private	Private
Benjamin A.	Allen	K	Sergeant	Sergeant
C. G.	Allen	E	Private	Private
G. Washington	Allen	I	Private	Private
George P.	Allen	I	Private	Private
George W.	Allen	G	Private	Private
George W.	Allen	I	Private	Private
J.	Allen	E	Private	Private
J. M.	Allen	E	Private	Private
Malaciah	Allen	E	Private	Second Lieutenant
N. L.	Allen	I	Private	Private
T. W.	Allen		Private	Private
W. Y.	Allen	I	Private	Private
William P.	Allen	G	Private	Private
James P.	Alman	I	Private	Private
J. P.	Almon	I	Private	Private
George P.	Almond	I	Private	Private
James M.	Alsup	C	Private	Private
G. D.	Ammonds	E	Private	Private
G. D.	Ammons	E	Private	Private
H. H.	Anderson	B	Private	Private

J. N.	Anderson	I	Private	Private
J. W.	Andrews	I	Private	Private
John N.	Andrews	I	Private	Private
Jefferson	Anglier	E	Private	Private
John S.	Anglin	K	Private	Private
William L.	Applewhite	F	Sergeant	First Lieutenant
Woods I. L.	Applewhite	F	Sergeant	First Lieutenant
Woodward S.	Applewhite	F	Sergeant	First Lieutenant
G. B.	Arbuckle	D	Private	Private
Daniel	Arendale	D	Private	Private
G. B.	Arendale	D	Private	Private
James R.	Arledge	H	Private	Private
William M.	Arledge	H	Private	Private
William M.	Arlege	H	Private	Private
William M.	Arlige	H	Private	Private
I.	Arnol	E	Private	Private
Isam H.	Arnold	E	Private	Private
James	Arnold	G	Private	Private
Elijah T.	Ashcroft	E	Private	Private
Alfred	Ashley	L	Private	Private
A.S.	Ashmore	D	Private	Private
Joshua B.	Ashmore	D	Private	Private
H.H.	Atkinson	E	Private	Private
Henry	Atkinson	E	Private	Private
Samuel A.	Averett	H	Sergeant	Private
S.A.	Avrett	A	Sergeant	Private
Charles B.	Bailey	D	Private	Private
Finis E.	Bailey	I	Private	Private
John Benton	Bailey	I	Private	Sergeant
Thomas J.	Bailey	D	Private	Second Lieutenant
G.L.	Bailis	A	Private	Private
L.B.	Baily	I	Private	Sergeant
Amos L.	Baker	K	Private	Private
James	Baker	C	Private	
Joseph	Baker	G	Private	
Antonio	Baptiste	L	Private	First Sergeant
Vincent	Baptiste	L	Private	Private
George W.	Barber	H	Private	Private
G.W.	Barbor	H	Private	Private
Richard W.	Barden	C	Private	Private

R.W.	Bardin	C	Private	Private
A.	Barlow	A	Corporal	Corporal
M.C.	Barton	B	Private	Private
James	Batson	G	Corporal	Corporal
Lorenzo	Batson	G	Private	Private
Thomas J.	Batson	G	Private	Private
J. Richard	Baugh	F	Third Lieutenant	Captain
Joel R.	Baugh	F	Third Lieutenant	Captain
Wm. L.	Baugh	F	Third Lieutenant	Captain
J. M.	Baylis	B	Second Lieutenant	Second Lieutenant
D. C.	Beachamp	E	Private	Private
J. W.	Beachamp	E	Private	Private
John W.	Beard	C	Private	Private
George	Beardslee	L	Private	Private
J. W.	Beauchamp	E	Private	Private
James A.	Beel	D	Private	Private
E. O.	Begers	C	Private	Private
William	Belcher	C	Private	Private
J.	Bell	A	Private	Musician
James	Bell	D	Private	Private
James A.	Bell	D	Private	Private
James McD.	Bell	D	Private	Private
James Q.	Bell	D	Private	Private
M. D.	Bell	D	Private	Private
Thomas J.	Bell	E	Private	Private
William	Bell	B	Private	Private
W.	Belland	B	Private	Private
B. G.	Benge	H		
E. M.	Bennett	A	Private	Private
Calvin W.	Benton	D	Private	Private
H. T.	Benton	D	Private	Private
W. A.	Benton	D	Private	Private
J. C.	Betterton	H	Private	Private
J. W.	Beuchamp	E	Private	Private
Ezekiel Q.	Biggeres	C	Private	Private
Thomas B.	Bigham	C	Private	Private
Bartlett S.	Bird	G	Private	Private
J. S.	Bird	D	Private	Private
John L.	Bishop	K	Sergeant	Sergeant
W. Ira	Bishop	K	Private	Private

William I.	Bishop	K	Private	Private
Alexander	Black	G	Corporal	First Sergeant
W. J.	Black	F	Private	Private
William C.	Black	G	Private	Sergeant
B. F.	Blackman	E	Private	Private
Samuel B.	Blackman	E	Private	Private
Solomon B.	Blackman	E	Private	Private
William G.	Blackman	L	Private	Private
B.F.	Blackmon	E	Private	Private
S.B.	Blackmon	E	Private	Private
B.F.	Blackwell	F	Private	Private
Benjamin F.	Blackwell	F	Private	Private
D.C.	Blackwell	F	Private	Private
J.M.	Blackwell	B	Private	Private
John W.	Blackwell	B	Private	Private
John Wesley	Blackwell	B	Private	Private
Waid	Blackwell	H	Private	Private
Wayne	Blackwell	H	Private	Private
William	Blackwell	B	Private	Private
R.C.	Blailoch	E	Private	Private
C.B.	Blanton	A	Private	Private
C.H.	Blanton	A	Private	Private
Charles M.	Blanton	A	Private	Private
W.H.	Blanton	A	Private	Private
M. T.	Blocker	E	Private	Private
Joseph H.	Bloodworth	D	Private	Private
David	Blue	H	Private	Private
David	Blue	H	Private	Private
John C.	Blue	H	Private	Private
A. J.	Boddie	H	Private	Private
Allen	Boddie	H	Private	Private
Augustus	Boddie	H	Private	Private
John	Bogne	C	Private	Private
J.	Bogue	C	Private	Private
M. J.	Bolan	F&S	Surgeon	Surgeon
W. J.	Bolan	F&S	Surgeon	Surgeon
William A.	Boman	H	Corporal	Corporal
Thomas A.	Bonner	K	Private	Private
J. T.	Boone	I	Sergeant	Sergeant
Benjamin H.	Booth	K	Private	Private

James M.	Booth	C	Corporal	Corporal
William P.	Booth	G	Senior Second Lieutenant	Second Lieutenant
G. W.	Bostick	A	Private	Private
L. C.	Bostick	A	Private	Private
S. C.	Bostick	A	Private	Private
Austin	Bounds	H	Corporal	Corporal
William A.	Bounds	H	Corporal	Corporal
Jesse	Bounnds	H	Private	Private
William A.	Bowans	H	Corporal	Corporal
Chesley	Bowen	F	Private	Private
William A.	Bowman	H	Corporal	Corporal
Jesse	Bownds	H	Private	Private
Jefferson	Box	C	Private	Private
Jeptha	Box	C	Private	Private
John L.	Boyd	E	First Sergeant	Captain
John T.	Boyd	E	Sergeant	First Sergeant
Joseph A.	Boyd	E	Private	Private
William C.	Boyd	E	Private	Private
George	Boyles	H	Private	Private
James	Boyles	H	Private	Private
John M.	Boyles	F&S	Second Lieutenant	Acting Commissary of Subsistence
Thomas	Boyles	K	Private	Private
Henry B.	Bradford	K	Private	Private
Henry B.	Bradford	K	Private	Private
John D.	Bradford	K	Private	Private
Calvin A.	Bradley	G	Private	Corporal
F. A.	Bradley	G	Private	Corporal
W.	Bradley	C	Private	Private
John	Brady	A	Private	Private
William M.	Brady	D	Private	Private
William M.	Braidy	D	Private	Private
J. W.	Braiziel	H	Private	Private
William R.	Bramble	C	Private	Corporal
W. M.	Brame	H	First Lieutenant	First Lieutenant
W. R.	Brandall	C	Private	Corporal
William R.	Brandle	C	Private	Corporal
Bryant T.	Brannan	L	Private	Private
Bryan T.	Brannon	L	Private	Private
Bryant T.	Branson	L	Private	Private

William	Brazeel	H	Private	Private
John W.	Braziel	H	Private	Private
William	Brazille	H	Private	Private
T.T.	Breeland	G	Private	Private
T. T.	Breland	G	Private	Private
W. H.	Brenton	C	Private	Private
A. L.	Bridges	A	Private	Private
G. P.	Bridges	E	Private	Private
P. C.	Bridges	A	Sergeant	Sergeant
H.	Brisclair	F	Private	Private
J. C.	Brittain	I	Private	Private
Qudellas W.	Brock	K	Private	Private
A. P.	Brown	A	Private	Private
Alexander A.	Brown	D	Privatc	Private
James H.	Brown	D	Private	Second Lieutenant
Philander P.	Brown	D	Brevet Second Lieutenant	First Lieutenant
William H.	Brown	I	Private	Private
Enoch G.	Browning	C	Private	Private
J.	Browning	C	Private	Private
T. T.	Bruland	G	Private	Private
William H.	Bruton	C	Private	Private
F. Y.	Bryan	I	Private	Corporal
Josiah E.	Bryan	K	Private	Private
T. A.	Bryan	I	Private	Private
Josiah E.	Bryant	K	Private	Private
Thomas A.	Bryant	I	Private	Private
William H.	Bryant	B	Private	Private
J. L.	Bryce	E	Private	Private
J. T.	Bryce	E	Private	Private
Calven E.	Buchanan	C	Private	Private
D. R.	Buchanan	H	Private	Private
J. W.	Buchanan	C	Sergeant	Sergeant
John A.	Buchanan	H	Private	Sergeant
W.	Buchanan	C	Private	Private
C. E.	Buchannon	C	Private	Private
John W.	Buckhanan	C	Sergeant	Sergeant
William	Buckhanan	C	Private	Private
J. S.	Buckner	F&S	Private	Assistant Surgeon
Joseph	Buckner	F&S	Private	Assistant Surgeon

John Lewis	Buffkin	H	Sergeant	Sergeant
John L.	Bufkin	H	Sergeant	Sergeant
Oliver I.	Bufkin	H	Private	Private
Oliver P.	Bufkin	H	Private	
Alexander P.	Buist	L	Corporal	Corporal
James H.	Bull	D	Private	Private
Henry H.	Bullock	F	Private	Private
William J.	Bullock	F	Private	Private
Edward	Bunkeson	L	Private	Private
A.L.	Burk	C	Private	Private
J.	Burk	C	Private	Private
J.P.	Burk	C	Private	Private
A.L.	Burke	C	Private	Private
Samuel J.	Burkes	I	Sergeant	Sergeant
Alfred	Burkhalter	F	Private	Private
Edward	Burkhalter	F	Private	Private
George W.	Burkhalter	F	Private	Private
William	Burkhalter	F	Private	Private
Alvin L.	Burks	C	Private	Private
J.	Burks	C	Private	Private
John P.	Burks	C	Private	Private
L.A. Jackson	Burks	I	Sergeant	Sergeant
Lemuel A.J.	Burks	I	Sergeant	Sergeant
Edward	Burleson	L	Private	Private
M. C.	Burnes	E	Private	Private
Andrew J.	Burns	C	Private	Private
H. J.	Burns	C	Private	Private
J. C.	Burns	I	Brevet Second Lieutenant	Second Lieutenant
M. C.	Burns	E	Private	Private
Michael C.	Byrnes	E	Private	Private
M. V.	Cagle	E	Private	Private
M. V.	Caigle	E	Private	Private
Richard A.	Cain	E	Private	Private
James A.	Caldar	C	Private	Private
John H.	Caldar	C	Private	Private
James A.	Calder	C	Private	Private
John H.	Calder	C	Private	Private
J. W.	Callis	G	Private	Private
James A.	Camnell	F&S	Captain	Colonel

Oscar F.	Camp	K	Private	Private
Edwin	Campbell	D	Private	Private
J. D.	Campbell	F&S	Captain	Colonel
James A.	Campbell	F&S	Captain	Colonel
R. F.	Campbell	H	Private	Private
S. A.	Campbell	G	Second Lieutenant	
Thomas	Campbell	H	Private	Private
Thomas H.	Canty	L	Private	Private
J. T.	Carley	G	Corporal	Corporal
James A.	Carnell	E	Captain	Colonel
Aquilla S.	Carnes	C	Private	Private
S.	Carnes	C	Private	Private
C.	Carnon	E	Private	Private
Aquillar S.	Carns	C	Private	Private
James M.	Carns	C	Private	Private
Thomas W.	Carr	K	Private	Private
Grief	Carroll	L	Private	Private
J.	Carroll	L	Private	Private
Jesse	Carroll	K	Private	Private
Samuel	Carroll	L	Private	Private
William J.	Carroll	C	Private	Private
Abner	Carter	G	Private	Private
Calvin P.E.	Carter	F	Private	Private
G.B.	Carter	G	Private	Private
G.N.	Carter	G	Sergeant	Sergeant
G.U.	Carter	G	Sergeant	Sergeant
John P.	Carter	G	Sergeant Major	Second Lieutenant
Samuel	Carter	L	Private	Private
Thomas C.	Carter	B	Private	Corporal
John W.	Carter, Jr.	G	Private	Private
John W.	Carter, Sr.	G	Private	Private
William H.	Cashion	K	Private	Private
Joel P.	Cato	E	Private	Sergeant
W. B.	Cato	E	Private	Private
William	Cato	E	Private	Private
Z. A.	Cato	E	Private	Private
Drury A.	Causby	K	Private	Private
J.N.	Chain	B	Private	Private
Joseph B.	Chain	F	Private	Private
Albert M.	Chambers	I	Corporal	Corporal

O.F.	Chambers	F	Private	Private
Robert	Chambers	I	Private	Private
William	Chandler	A	Private	Private
Palo	Charles	B	Private	Private
C.C.	Chatam	B	Private	Private
Claiborn	Chatham	B	Private	Private
Joseph A.	Cheap	K	Private	Private
Joseph A.	Cheech	K	Private	Private
James H.	Check	K	Private	Private
James Henry	Cheek	K	Private	Private
Joseph A.	Cheek	K	Private	Private
A.	Chesser	A	Private	Private
J.H.	Childers	G	Second Lieutenant	Second Lieutenant
J.W.	Childress		Private	Private
George B.	Chisman	H	Private	Private
John W.	Christopher	A	Private	First Sergeant
R.C.	Clafton	K	Private	Private
I.A.	Clain	C	Private	Private
Charles A.	Clark	L	Private	Private
John	Clark	G	Private	Private
Richard	Clayton	K	Private	Private
Patrick H.	Clifton	C	Private	Private
D. G.	Cochran	H	Private	Private
Frank B.	Cochran	H	Private	Private
Samuel D.	Cochran	H	Private	
T. R.	Cochran	H	Private	Private
J. D.	Cockeroft	E	Private	Private
James	Cockeroft	E	Private	Private
William H.	Coe	C	Private	Private
W. B.	Colbert	E	Private	First Lieutenant
J. C.	Cole	I	Private	Private
S. C.	Cole	I	Private	Private
James K.	Coleman	I	Private	Corporal
James S. L.	Colley	K	Private	Private
James R.	Collins	C	Private	Private
T. E.	Collins	G	Private	Private
James S. L.	Colly	K	Private	Private
James	Colmes	E	Private	Private
Andrew J.	Conn	C	Private	Private
J. M.	Conn	C	Private	Private

William F.	Conn	C	Private	Corporal
William T.	Conn	C	Private	Corporal
Edward	Cook	E	Private	Private
W. K.	Cook	E	Private	Private
Elias	Cooley	H	Private	Private
Henry J.	Cooley	H	Private	Private
John W.	Cooley	H	Private	Private
William	Cooley	H	Private	Private
James M.	Cooly	H	Private	Private
John W.	Cooly	H	Private	Private
Hiram	Cooper	B	Private	Private
Nathan	Cooper	B	Private	Private
Norval	Cooper	B	Corporal	Second Lieutenant
Drury A.	Cosby	K	Private	Private
A.H.	Cotton	E	Private	Private
B.J.F.	Cotton	E	Private	Private
W.F.	Cowan	C	Private	Corporal
W.T.	Cowan	C	Private	Corporal
W.S.	Cowley	K	Private	Private
William S.	Cowly	K	Private	Private
William S.	Cown	C	Private	Corporal
Richard C.	Cox	C	Private	Private
Rufus J.	Cox	K	Private	Private
William C.	Cox	C	Private	Sergeant
William H.	Cox	C	Private	Private
William R.	Cox	C	Private	Sergeant
Benjamin P.	Crabb	E	Private	Private
Add	Craft	F&S	Captain	Acting Quartermaster
And.	Craft	F&S	Captain	Acting Quartermaster
N.O.	Craft	F	Brevet Second Lieutenant	Second Lieutenant
Thomas J.	Craft	F	Private	Sergeant
A.J.	Crain	C	Private	Private
J.H.	Crain	C	Private	Private
Joshua A.	Crain	C	Private	Private
William	Cramp	F&S	Adjutant	Lieutenant/Adjutant
Joshua A.	Crane	C	Private	Private
R.	Crane	E	Private	Private
Albert S.	Craven	L	Private	Private
J.H.	Crebbs	L	Private	Private

Columbus	Creel	B	Private	Private
Ella	Creel	B	Private	Private
Isiah	Creel	B	Private	Private
James T.	Creel	B	Private	Private
Columbus	Creil	B	Private	Private
W.	Crisnell	D	Private	Private
William	Criszelle	D	Private	Private
T.J.	Croft	F	Private	Sergeant
Conrad	Croma	L	Private	Private
W.B.	Crosthwait	D	Corporal	Corporal
W.M.	Crowder	E	Private	Private
W.R.	Crowder	E	Private	Private
William H.	Crowder	E	Private	Private
Conrad	Crowmar	L	Private	Private
Ella	Crul	B	Private	Private
I.	Crul	B	Private	Private
J.R.	Crul, Jr.	B	Musician	Private
J.R.	Crul, Sr.	B	Corporal	Corporal
William	Crumm	C	Private	Private
William	Crump	F&S	Adjutant	Lieutenant/Adjutant
Francis	Cunningham	L	Private	Private
S.A.	Cunningham	L	Private	Private
Simon	Cunningham	L	Private	Private
Cortez H.	Currie	E	Private	Private
Neal D.	Currie	D,E	Private	Private
R.E.	Currie	E	Private	Private
H.H.	Dagan	D	Private	Sergeant
John	Dagler	E	Private	Private
Oliver	Dale	H	Private	Private
John N.	Danial	A	Private	Private
J.A.	Daniel	A	Private	
J.N.	Daniel	A	Private	Private
S.H.	Daniel	A	Private	Private
Oliver S.	Dase	H	Private	Private
J. S.	Daton	C	Private	Private
Barnes G.	Daughtry	K	Private	Private
Adalando D.	Daves	C	Private	Private
A. D.	Davis	C	Private	Private
Edward	Davis	E	Private	Private
H. D.	Davis	E	Private	Private

J. L.	Davis	A	Private	Private
James R.	Davis	G	Private	Private
R. C.	Davis	A	Private	Private
R. T.	Davis	E	Private	Sergeant
Robert	Davis	A	Private	Private
T. R.	Davis	E	Private	Sergeant
John S.	Dayton	C	Private	Private
George L.	DeWitt	F	Private	Private
A.	Dean	C	Private	Private
James H.	Dean	K	Private	Private
O. S.	Dean	H	Private	Private
William F.	Dean	K	Private	Private
William S.	Dean	L	Private	Private
Charles T.	Dease	D	Private	Private
Geo. F.	Dease	H	Private	
Oliver S.	Dease	H	Private	Private
John S.	Deaton	C	Private	Private
William R.	Deaton	C	Private	Private
Charles F.	Dees	D	Private	Private
Alfred A.	Deese	D	Private	Private
Charles F.	Deese	D	Private	Private
Culpeper W.	Deese	D	Private	Private
George D.	Delancy	B	Private	Private
J.B.	Delancy	B	Private	Private
Valentine	Delany	L	Private	Private
Morris	Delmas	L	Private	Private
Valentine	Delmas	L	Private	Private
G.B.	Denham	G	First Lieutenant	First Lieutenant
E.	Denson	E	Private	Private
J.W.	Dewalt		Private	Private
John L.	Dewitt	F	Private	Private
L.L.	Dewitt	F	Private	Private
William L.	Dewitt	F	Private	Private
J.	Dickey	B	Private	Private
J.H.	Dickson	E	Private	Private
W.B.	Dikes	F	Private	Private
J.A.	Dillard	C	Private	Private
John T.	Dillard	C	Private	Private
J.T.	Dilliard	C	Private	Private
H.C.	Dismuke	E	Private	Private

Theodore F.	Dismuke	E	Private	Private
K.C.	Divine	F&S	Surgeon	Surgeon
Ezechial	Dixon	G	Private	Private
Alfred	Dobson	G	Private	Private
Edmund	Dodson	L	Private	Private
Hamilton H.	Dogan	D	Private	Sergeant
Hunter H.	Dogan	D	Private	Sergeant
James A.	Dogan	D	Corporal	Corporal
James Alford	Dogan	D	Corporal	Corporal
James H.	Dogan	D	Corporal	Corporal
F. M.	Dorsey	B	Private	Private
E. D.	Dossett	B	Private	Private
Edmond	Dossett	B	Private	Private
Francis M.	Dossett	B	Private	Private
Hansford D.	Dossett	B	Private	Private
James A.	Dossett	B	Private	Private
B.F.	Doughton	D	Private	Private
J.J.	Dowling	H	Private	Private
James A.E.	Dowling	H	Private	Hospital Steward
J.A.	Downs	L	Drummer	Drum Major
Jack	Downs	L	Drummer	Drum Major
Jabas	Drake	E	Private	Private
G.S.	Draughan	G	Private	Private
Griffin S.	Draughn	G	Private	Private
W.J.	Draughn	G	Private	Private
J.E.	Dreak	C	Private	Private
J.E.	Dreke	C	Private	Private
J.P.	Dreury	C	Private	Private
J.P.	Drewry	C	Private	Private
J.P.	Drury	C	Private	Private
Daniel A.	Duff	C	Private	Private
John L.	Duitt	F	Private	Private
William L.	Duitt	F	Private	Private
John H.	Duke	D	Private	Corporal
Edward	Dumassail		Private	Private
S.	Dunlap	F	Private	Private
Henry H.	Dunn	F	Corporal	Private
Alfred E.	Dupont	L	Private	Private
Alfred Edward	Dupont	L	Private	Private
E. A.	Dupont	L	Private	Private

Louis J.	Dupont	L	Private	Private
Lucien	Dupont	L	Private	Private
William	Dupont	L	Private	Private
A.E.	Dusson	I	Private	Private
John	Dyess	B	Private	Private
D.S.	Dykes	G	Private	Private
Henry C.	Dykes	F	Private	Private
W.B.	Dykes	F	Private	Private
William	Dykes	F	Private	Private
Gilead A.	Eady	I	Private	Private
A. B.	Easterling	G	Private	
Andrew J.	Easterling	B	Private	Private
J. M.	Easterling	B	Private	Private
James B.	Easterling	B	Private	Private
A. J.	Eastridge	D	Private	Private
John N.	Eaton	F	Private	Private
William Jasper	Eaton	F	First Lieutenant	First Lieutenant
George C.	Echols	C	Private	Private
James M.	Echols	C	Private	Private
William E.	Echols	C	Private	Private
William	Eddins	H	Private	Private
G. A.	Eddy	I	Private	Private
Hiram C.	Edge	K	Private	Private
William	Edmondson	B	Private	Sergeant
William	Edmonson	B	Private	Sergeant
George R.	Edwards	E	Private	Private
J. M.	Edwards	A	Private	Private
James M.	Edwards	E	Private	First Lieutenant
Jesse M.	Edwards	L	Private	Private
Lucius Q.	Edwards	E	Corporal	Corporal
M. C.	Edwards	E	Second Lieutenant	First Lieutenant
Senale	Edwards	G	Private	Private
Fedick	Ehlers	L	Private	Private
Henry	Ehlers	L	Private	Private
Henry	Ehners	L	Private	Private
Frederick	Ekleis	L	Private	Private
Joseph	Ellenberg	I	Private	Private
G.	Ellett	C	Private	Private
G.	Elliot	C	Private	Private
Charles	Ellis	L	Private	Private

Frederic	Ellis	L	Private	Private
Henry	Ellis	L	Private	Private
William	Ellis	L	Private	Private
Green	Ellot	C	Private	Private
Henry	Elmers	L	Private	Private
J.	Elzey	B	Private	Private
Isaac	Enloe	E	Private	Private
Reuben	Estes	I	First Sergeant	Private
Francis M.	Evans	K	Private	Private
Joseph H.	Evans	A	Private	Corporal
Milton	Evans	L	Private	Private
William B.	Evans	K	First Lieutenant	First Lieutenant
James	Evens	A	Private	Private
Joseph H.	Evens	A	Private	Corporal
Absalom	Faggard	L	Private	Private
Cicero	Fail	G	Private	Private
A.W.	Failes	H	Private	Private
Alexander W.	Fairley	G	Private	Private
John C.	Fairley	G	Private	Private
P.H.	Fairley	G	Private	Sergeant
William S.	Fairley	G	Private	Private
F.	Faler	F	Private	Private
Benjamin A.	Faris	D	Sergeant	Private
Newton I.	Faris	D	Private	Private
Peter H.	Farley	G	Private	Sergeant
C.	Farmer	F	Private	Private
James	Farmer	F	Private	Private
Thomas C.	Farr	K	Private	Private
Benjamin A.	Farris	D	Sergeant	Private
N.I.	Farris	D	Private	Private
Obediah C.	Fatheree	H	Private	Private
James M.	Fears	K	Private	Private
William	Fergurson	E	Private	Sergeant
Archibald	Ferguson	H,B	Private	Private
Daniel	Ferguson	H	Private	Private
L.	Ferguson	M	Private	Private
William M.	Ferguson	E	Private	Sergeant
Gabriel	Feurd	C	Private	Private
P.	Fewall	B	Private	Private
J.M.	Fewok	B	Private	Private

J.M.	Fewox	B	Private	Private
W. L.	Fillingame	H	Private	Private
John	Finley	H	Private	Private
Henry J.	Fisher	I	Private	Private
Isaac N.	Fisher	E	Private	Private
Lewis H.	Fisher	L	Private	Private
Lucius A.	Fisher	E	Private	Private
H. J.	Fishes	I	Private	Private
F.N.	Flowers	A	Private	Private
J. A.	Flowers	I	Private	Private
John A.	Flowers	A	Private	Private
Joshua A.	Flowers	A	Private	Private
Peter	Flynn	E	Private	Private
Gabriel	Foard	C	Private	Private
C. D.	Fontain	C	Private	Private
George	Forbes	I	Private	Private
George	Forbus	I	Private	Private
Henry	Forbus	I	Private	Private
Gabriel	Ford	C	Private	Private
John F.	Ford	E	Private	Private
Charles D.	Fountain	C	Private	Private
J. W.	Fowler	A	Corporal	Brevet Second Lieutenant
James	Fowler	D	Private	Private
R. W.	Fox	E	Private	Private
Aring I.	France	C	Private	Private
B.	Franks	C	Private	Private
Henry E. N.	Franks	C	Private	Private
Henry G.	Franks	C	Private	Private
Edward	Frasier	E	Private	Private
Edward	Frazer	E	Private	Private
Edward	Frazier	E	Private	Private
Louis J.	Frederic	L	Private	Sergeant
Hezakiah D.	Freeland	E	Private	Private
Hiram A.	Freeland	L	Private	Private
J. C.	Freeman	G	Private	Private
William R.	Freeman	G	Private	Private
R. J.	Freeny	E	Private	Private
H. D.	Freland	E	Private	Private
W. H.	Freland	E	Private	Private

Ervin D.	French	A	Private	Private
W. M.	French	D	Private	Private
William H.	French	D	Private	Private
R. C.	Freney	E	Private	Private
R. J.	Freney	E	Private	Private
Jonah W.	Friday	A	Private	Corporal
Reuben	Friday	A	Private	Private
W. B.	Fulks	C	Private	Private
Daniel	Furgerson	H	Private	Private
William M.	Furgerson	E	Private	Sergeant
Archibald	Furguson	H,B	Private	Private
John G.	Futch		Private	Private
Robert J.	Futch		Private	Private
James W.	Gable	H	Musician	Private
J. W.	Galaspy	E	Private	Private
J. W.	Galespy	E	Private	Private
A.	Gandy	B	Private	Private
E. M.	Gandy	B	Private	Private
John J.	Gandy	B	Private	Private
Meshock M.	Gandy	B	Private	Private
Noel	Gandy	B	Private	Private
M. M.	Ganly	B	Private	Private
Benjamin F.	Garaway	G,E	Private	Private
J. R.	Garaway	G	Private	Private
German	Gardner	H	Private	Private
John C.	Gardner	H	Private	Private
William	Gardner	H	Private	Private
James	Garner	D	Private	Private
J. M.	Garrison	C	Private	Private
J. N.	Garrison	C	Private	Private
Joseph A.	Garrison	C	Private	Private
B. F.	Garroway	G,E	Private	Private
Mitchell	Gatlin	H	Private	Private
E. M.	Gaudy	B	Private	Private
J. J.	Gaudy	B	Private	Private
M. M.	Gaudy	B	Private	Private
N.	Gaudy	B	Private	Private
J.P.	Gaynes	I	Private	Private
James W.	Gellespie	E	Private	Private
John	Gellespie	E	Private	Private

Benjamin F.	Gibson	K	Private	Private
William	Gibson	G	Private	Private
James F.	Gillam	I	Private	Private
James H.	Gilliam	C	Private	Private
William E.	Gilliam	C	Private	Private
E.M.	Gillis	G	Corporal	Corporal
Samuel H.	Gist	G	Private	Second Lieutenant
John F.	Gladney	K	Private	Private
John S.	Gladney	K	Private	Private
John H.	Goff	L	Private	Sergeant
Joseph	Goff	L	Private	Private
William	Goff	L	Private	Private
William W.	Goff	L	Private	Private
William Wiley	Goff	H,L	Private	Private
Samuel	Goleman	G	Private	Private
Gideon J.	Gooch	D	Private	Private
H.H.	Goodwin	A	Private	Private
J.K.	Goodwin	C	Private	Private
J.	Gordon	B	Private	Private
Milton	Gordy	G	Private	Private
William W.	Gough	D	Private	Private
George C.	Grace	D	Private	Corporal
Oliver G.	Gracey	H	Private	Private
John A.	Grady	K	Private	Private
David	Graham	E,B	Private	Private
David	Graham	M	Private	Private
James S.	Graham	H	Private	Private
John Q.	Graham	H	Private	Private
Laird	Graham	L	Private	Private
S.F.	Graham	H	Private	Private
S.G.	Graham	H,L	Private	Private
S.S.	Graham	H,L	Private	Private
W. L.	Graham	C	Private	Private
W.L.	Graham	E	Private	Private
William	Graham	L	Private	Private
William N.G.	Graham	L	Private	Private
S.J.	Grahan	H,L	Private	Private
John C.	Grant	L	Private	Corporal
Richard	Grantham	G	Private	Private
Oliver G.	Grason	H	Private	Private

J. F.	Gray	E	Private	Private
D. B.	Grayham	E,B	Private	Private
E. B.	Grayham	E	Private	Private
James W.	Grayson	B	Third Lieutenant	Second Lieutenant
John W.	Grayson	B	Sergeant	Sergeant
Oliver G.	Grayson	H	Private	Private
Enoch	Green	I	Private	Private
John W.	Green	I	Private	Private
S. W.	Green	I	Private	Private
W. J.	Green	I	Private	
Frederic	Greenaugh	L	Private	Private
Frederic	Greenhoe	L	Private	Private
Erasmus F.	Griffin	L	Private	Private
H. Bruno	Griffin	L	Captain	Captain
Hiram B.	Griffin	L	Captain	Captain
Ira P.	Griffith	A	Private	Private
William	Griggs	I	Private	Private
Edward C.	Grimes	H	Private	Private
Eldred C.	Grimes	H	Private	Private
Francis	Grimes	L	Private	Private
G. M. D.	Grisham	C	Private	Private
Richard A.	Grisham	C	Private	Private
Wilson P.	Grizzle	K	Corporal	Corporal
John	Groves	E	Private	Private
James M.	Grubbs	B	Private	Private
T. A.	Guinness	I	Private	Corporal
John	Gunn	I	Private	Private
J. M.	Gunter	B	Private	Private
Eli H.	Guthrie	I	Private	Private
M. W.	Guthrie	I	Private	Private
J. P.	Guynes	I	Private	Private
T. A.	Guynes	I	Private	Corporal
Louis	Habbuman	K	Private	Private
Louis	Haberman	K	Private	Private
Samuel J.	Hagan	L	Private	Private
Alexander	Hale	C	Private	Private
Charles M. H.	Hale	C	Private	Private
Emanuel N.	Hale	C	Private	Private
James B.	Hale	C	Private	Private
Jeremiah H.	Hale	C	Corporal	Corporal

Joel H.	Hale	C	Private	Private
Joel	Hale Jr.	C	Private	Private
Green B.	Haley	I	Private	Private
A.	Hall	E	Private	Private
Alexander	Hall	C	Private	Private
C. W.	Hall	A	Private	Private
Edward	Hall	H	Private	Private
R. J.	Hall	E	Private	Private
W. Wood	Hall	D	First Lieutenant	Captain
William J.	Hall	K	Private	Private
William W.	Hall	D	First Lieutenant	Captain
Richard	Halverston	L	Corporal	Corporal
Nicholas	Hamel	L	Private	Private
Nicholas	Hamlet	L	Private	Private
W.J.	Hammuck	I	Private	Private
P. Columbus	Hancock	I	Private	Private
T.G.	Hancock	1	Private	Private
J. H.	Hanks	D	Private	Private
William M.	Hanks	D	Private	Sergeant
E. B.	Hanna	A	Private	Private
C. B.	Hannah	A	Private	Private
S. S.	Hannah	A	Private	Private
Thomas L.	Hannah	A	First Sergeant	Second Lieutenant
William M. Jr.	Hannah	A	Brevet Second Lieutenant	First Lieutenant
Barnabas L.	Hannigan	F	Private	Corporal
H. H.	Hanson	E	Private	Private
Kindred	Hardee	H	Private	Private
L. S.	Hardon	E	Private	Private
Kindred	Hardy	H	Private	Private
William	Hargrave	C	Private	Private
W. M. N.	Hargroves	C	Private	Private
William N.	Hargroves	C	Private	Private
J. A.	Harns	C	Private	Private
John M.	Harper	E	Private	Private
William T.	Harper	E	Private	Sergeant
J.	Harrell	B	Private	Private
J.	Harrell	E	Private	Private
Thomas J.	Harrell	B	Private	Private
Thomas J.	Harriel	B	Private	Private

R.	Harries	E	Private	Private
J. C.	Harrin	B	Private	Private
A. W.	Harrington	D	Private	Private
Mathew	Harris	D	Private	Corporal
Reuben	Harris	E	Private	Private
William	Harris	B	Private	Private
B. F.	Harrison	E	Private	Private
Benjamin H.	Harrison	E	Private	Private
Thomas J.	Harrold	B	Private	Private
Joseph	Hart	E	Private	Private
Louis	Hart	E	Private	Private
Green V.	Hasley	I	Private	Private
Green V.	Hastly	I	Private	Private
John G.	Hathorn	F	Private	Private
William W.	Hathorn	F	Private	Sergeant
G.V.	Hausley	I	Private	Private
William	Havard	L	Private	Private
Lewis	Haverman	K	Private	Private
Charles R.	Hawkins	L	Private	Private
David K.	Hawkins	L	Private	Private
David R.	Hawkins	L	Private	Private
Felix G.	Hawkins	K	Private	
Thomas K.	Hawkins	L	First Lieutenant	First Lieutenant
William H.	Hawkins	L	Private	Private
J.C.	Hawthorne	F	Private	Private
A.J.	Hays	F&S	Lieutenant Colonel	Lieutenant Colonel
E.	Hays	C	Private	Private
Robert M.	Hays	C	Private	Private
Thomas J.	Haziold	B	Private	Private
John A.	Hearns	C	Private	Private
Joshua C.	Hearns	C	Private	Private
Joseph	Heart	E	Private	Private
Lewis	Heart	E	Private	Private
James R.	Hedge	H	Private	Private
John C.	Heidelberg	H	Private	Private
Samuel S.	Heidelberg	H	Private	Private
Thomas C.	Heidelberg	H	Private	Sergeant
Washington I.	Heidelberg	H	Private	Private
John C.	Heidleburg	H	Private	Private

M.L.	Heidleburg	H	Private	Private
T.C.	Heidleburg	H	Private	Sergeant
W.I.	Heidleburg	H	Private	Private
P.	Helverson	B	Private	Private
Peter	Helverston	B	Private	Private
Peter	Helverston	L	Corporal	Sergeant
Richard	Helverston	L	Corporal	Corporal
James	Helveston	L	Private	Private
Peter	Helveston	B	Private	Private
Peter	Helveston	L	Corporal	Sergeant
Richard	Helveston	L	Corporal	Corporal
B.	Henderson	C	Private	Private
Samuel G.	Henderson	E	Private	Quartermaster Sergeant
William L.	Hendon	A	Second Lieutenant	Second Lieutenant
John A.	Hendricks	E	Private	Private
John M.	Hendricks	E	Private	Private
John N.	Hendricks	E	Private	Private
John W.	Hendricks	E	Private	Private
Marion J.	Hendricks	K	Private	Private
Henry C.	Hendrix	E	Private	Private
John W.	Hendrix	E	Private	Private
Marion J.	Hendrix	K	Private	Private
Barnabas L.	Henigan	F	Private	Corporal
Alexander L.	Henkle	E	Private	Private
William C.	Henley	K	Private	Private
William C.	Henly	K	Private	Private
Barney L.	Hennegan	F	Private	Corporal
Samuel A.	Hennigan	F	Sergeant	Sergeant
Barnabas L.	Hennington	F	Private	Corporal
Jasper	Henson	D	Private	Private
Richard	Henson	B	Private	Private
Thomas C.	Herdelbery	H	Private	Sergeant
Henry	Herley	C	Private	Private
John	Herndon	L	Private	Private
J.	Herrand	B	Private	Private
Samuel P.	Herrel	D	Private	Private
J.A.	Herrin	C	Private	Private
Jesse	Herrin	B	Private	Private
S.D.	Herrin	F	Private	Private

R.O.	Hester	B	Private	Private
Joseph J.	Hickey	C	Private	Private
D.H.	Hickman	H	Private	Private
James H.	Hickman	H	Private	Private
James M.	Hickman	H	Private	Private
John M.	Hickman	H	Private	Private
Joseph J.	Hicky	C	Private	Private
Washington I.	Hidelberg	H	Private	Private
Lauson G.	Higginbotham	C	Private	Private
T.E.	Hildebrand	I	Private	Private
Enbulus C.	Hill	E	Private	Sergeant
H.C.	Hill	E	Private	Private
J.N.	Hill	C	Private	Private
J.R.	Hill	B	Private	Private
James J.	Hill	F	Private	Private
Jesse W.	Hill	K	Corporal	Corporal
John	Hill	B	Private	Private
Mark B.	Hill	C	Sergeant	Sergeant
Marlin V.	Hill	B	Private	Private
Martin B.	Hill	C	Sergeant	Sergeant
Robert	Hill	B	Private	
Robert E.	Hill	K	Private	Private
Thomas	Hill	E	Private	Private
L.	Hindman	H		
Jasper	Hinson	D	Private	Private
A.J.	Hinton	G	Private	Private
James	Hinton	G	Private	Private
Prentiss	Hinton	G	Private	Private
John H.	Hobbs	D	Private	Private
W.H.	Hobbs	B	Private	Private
Peter	Hoben	E	Private	Private
P.E.	Hodge	H	Private	Private
Powhattan E.	Hodges	H	Private	Private
William P.	Hodges	H	Private	Private
S.S.	Hodnett	A	Private	Private
S.S.	Hodwitt	A	Private	Private
Lemuel J.	Hogan	L	Private	Private
Peter	Hogan	E	Private	Private
Samuel J.	Hogan	L	Private	Private
J.B.	Holder	G	Private	Private

Leonidas A.	Holeshouser	D	Private	Private
W.B.	Holeshouser	D	Private	Private
Elisha	Holland	A	Private	Private
W.J.	Holland	D	Private	Private
L.A.	Hollayhouse	D	Private	Private
Elisha	Hollen	A	Private	Private
Levi	Holliman	G	Private	Private
J.	Hollingsworth	G	Private	Private
Jacob	Hollinsworth	G	Private	Private
William	Hollis	K	Private	Private
W.J.	Holloway	F	First Sergeant	First Sergeant
W.D.	Holly	B	Private	Private
Leonidas A.	Holshouser	D	Private	Private
William	Holshouser	D	Private	Private
Colon	Hood	B	Private	Private
Anthony	Hook	L	Private	Private
H.	Hook	L	Private	Private
A.G.	Hooks	E	Private	Private
Green V.	Hoosley	I	Private	Private
B.G.	Horne	I	Private	Private
G.V.	Horsley	I	Private	Private
Green B.	Hosley	I	Private	Private
Green V.	Hosley	I	Private	Private
F.	Hough	B	Private	Private
F.	House	A	Private	Corporal
Leonard W.	House	A	Private	Corporal
Logan	House	A	Private	Private
Nicholas	House	A	Private	Private
George W.	Housley	G	Private	Private
Francis M.	Howard	H	Private	Private
Michael	Howard	C	Private	Private
George W.	Huckabee	C	Private	Private
G. W.	Huckybee	C	Private	Private
Samuel S.	Huddleberry	H	Private	Private
Samuel F.	Hudelburgh	H	Private	Private
John	Hudson	C	Private	Private
William B.	Hudson	I	Private	Private
William D.	Hudson	I	Private	Private
McDonald G.	Hughes	E	Private	Private
V. R.	Hughes	E	Private	Private

Timothy	Hughs	H		
W. E.	Humphries	I	Private	Private
Henry C.	Hunt	D	Private	Private
Pickens B.	Hunter	K	Private	Private
E. Orville	Huntley	A	Captain	Captain
M.C.	Huntley	A	First Lieutenant	First Lieutenant
W.C.	Huntley	A	First Lieutenant	First Lieutenant
W.C.	Huntley	A	Sergeant	Sergeant
William T.	Huntley	A	Musician	Musician
Henry J.	Hurley	C	Private	Private
G.W.	Hutchenson	D	Private	Private
G.W.	Hutchinson	D	Private	Private
George	Hutchinson	D	Private	Private
J.M.	Hutchinson	A	Private	Private
J.M.	Hutchison	A	Private	Private
M.	Hutchison	A	Private	Private
John	Hutson	C	Private	Private
James J.	Hyde	I	Private	Second Lieutenant
Jeff J.	Hyde	I	Private	Second Lieutenant
Jonathan J.	Inman	K	Private	Corporal
G.Y.	Irby	I	Private	Private
Calaway	Ivy	E	Private	Private
W. W.	Jackson	H	Private	Private
Warren W.	Jackson	H	Private	Private
William J.	Jackson	A	Private	Private
David M.	James	C	Private	Private
Isaac M.	James	C	Private	Private
Joel C.	James	I	Private	Private
Theophilus L.	James	C	Private	Private
William M.	James	C	Private	Private
James E.	Jarman	K	Private	Private
James Edgar	Jarman	K	Private	Private
Robert A.	Jarman	K	Private	Private
Henry	Jenkins	G	Private	Private
William H.	Jenkins	B	Private	Private
Allen	Johnson	E	Private	Private
Eriah A.	Johnson	B	Private	Private
H.S.	Johnson	E	Private	Private
J.H.	Johnson	E	Private	Private
James	Johnson	D	Private	Private

James H.	Johnson	I		John L.
James M.	Johnson	G		William J
James M.	Johnson	K		G.E.
James S.	Johnson	I		B.F.
Job	Johnson	I		W.J.
John	Johnson	C		William C
John	Johnson	H		B.F.
Joseph	Johnson	A		Reubin V
Samuel	Johnson	I		W.R.
Samuel M.	Johnson	I		William
Samuel W.	Johnson	L	Se	Willis
William	Johnson	A		William
William M.	Johnson	A		John M
Z.	Johnson	E		C.W.
Zachariah	Johnson	A		John Mor
F.L.	Joiner	C		Julius
A.A.	Jones	C		R.M.
A.O.	Jones	B		J.H.
A.S.	Jones	E		Nichol
A.S.	Jones	I	Firs	Alfre
Alfred	Jones	I		M.T.C
Amos O.	Jones	B		Steph
Andrew J.	Jones	C		S.
Ausborn O.	Jones	B		Andrev
Calvin D.	Jones	B	C	Freder
J.P.	Jones	G		Georg
John	Jones	E		J.F
John C.	Jones	H	F	John
Josephus M.B.	Jones	G	P	Thom
M.H.	Jones	I	P	Wil
R.C.	Jones	D	P	Isaac
Robert C.	Jones	K	P	Isaac
Robert E.	Jones	K	Pr	J.
Stephen	Jones	K	Pr	J.
Thomas M.	Jones	F&S	Co	H.
William	Jones	C	Pri	Abn
Joseph	Jonte	L	Pri	Nich
J.W.	Jordan	E	Pri	J.
John L.	Jordan	E	Serg	Al
William J.	Jordan	E	Priv	

	Name	Co.	Rank 1	Rank 2
	Jourdan	E	Sergeant	Private
	Jourdan	E	Private	Private
	Judson	E	Private	Private
	Keelin	DBE	Private	Private
	Keelin	D	Private	Private
	Keelin	D	Private	Private
	Keeling	DBE	Private	Private
	Kelly	F	Private	Private
	Kelly	F	Private	Private
	Kelly	A	Private	Private
	Kelly	A	Private	Private
	Kelshaw	L	Private	Private
	Kenedy	E	Private	Private
	Kennedy	I	Corporal	Corporal
roe	Kennedy	E	Private	Private
.	Kennedy	G	Captain	Captain
	Kennedy	E	Private	Private
	Kerbs	L	Private	Private
s	Kiersh	L	Private	Private
	Kilgore	I	Second Lieutenant	First Lieutenant
.	Kilgore	B	Private	Private
n	Kimbraugh	I	Private	Private
	Kimbrill	I	Private	Private
J.	Kinard	A	Private	Private
J.	Kinard	A	Private	Private
W.	King	C	Private	Private
	King	C	Corporal	Private
R.	King	C	Private	Brevet Second Lieutenant
s J.	King	C	Corporal	Private
y	King	A	Private	Private
M.	Kingman	A	Private	Sergeant
N.	Kingman	A	Private	Sergeant
	Kingman	A	Private	Corporal
	Kingman	K	Private	Sergeant
	Kinnaird	A	Private	Private
r B.	Kirk	H	Private	Private
las	Kirsh	L	Private	Private
.	Kite	I	Private	Private
ert	Knight	F	Private	Private

Daniel	Knight	F	Private	Private
Franklin	Knight	F	Private	Private
J.D.	Knight	B	Private	
James	Knight	B	Private	Corporal
Leonard L.	Knight	F	Private	Private
Aristide H.	Krebs	L	Junior Second Lieutenant	Brevet Second Lieutenant
Arthur R.	Krebs	L	Private	Private
Joseph H.	Krebs	L	Private	Private
C.	Krome	L	Private	Private
E.F.	Lacy	E	Private	Private
George W.	Lagrone	K	Private	Private
Nathan S.	Laird	F	Private	Private
John	Lambert	G	Private	Private
Thomas O.	Lambert	G	Private	Private
William	Lambert	G	Private	Private
Joseph	Lamden	H		
S.M.	Lane	D	Private	Private
Alexander M.	Langston	G,A	Private	Private
Frank M.	Lantrip	K	Private	Private
John B.	Lantrip	K	Private	Private
James L.	Lath	H	Private	Private
S.W.	Law	D	Private	Private
Alfred P.	Lawson	I	Private	Corporal
Alfred Pinckney	Lawson	I	Private	Corporal
William	Lea	I	Private	Private
B.F.	Lee	G	Private	Private
Bithae B.	Lee	H	Private	Private
ST.	Lee	I	Sergeant	Sergeant
W.P.	Lee	G	Private	Private
William	Lee	G	Private	Private
William F.	Leggett	F	Corporal	Corporal
Joseph	Lemaitre	L	Private	Private
J.	Lemater	L	Private	Private
Joseph	Lemetre	L	Private	Private
E.S.	Lenard	I	Private	Private
Frank J.	Leonard	G	Private	Private
Edward H.	Lewis	K	Private	Private
John L.	Lewis	K	Private	Private
P.C.	Lichtsey	H	Corporal	Corporal

B.C.	Light	H	Private	Private
Franklin J.	Lightsey	H	Private	Private
John C.L.	Lightsey	H	Private	Private
John Charles	Lightsey	H	Private	Private
Peter C.	Lightsey	H	Corporal	Corporal
Jas. R.	Linly	K	Private	
John	Lintz	L	Private	Private
John	Lipps	B	Private	Private
George H.	Lipscomb	F&S	Major	Major
John	Lipse	B	Private	Private
Thomas	Little	L	Private	Private
John	Litz	B	Private	Private
R.C.	Livingston	A	Private	Private
Thomas M.	Livingston	A	Private	Private
C.	Loeb	B	Private	Private
Lacail	Loeb	B	Private	Private
George A.	Loflin	F	Private	Private
James K.P.D.	Loflin	F	Private	Ensign
William H.	Logan	A	Private	Private
J.H.	Lonsing		Private	Private
Absalom J.	Lott	F	Private	Private
D.W.	Lott	F	Private	Private
G.W.	Lott	F	Sergeant	Sergeant
J.E.	Lott	F	Private	Private
J.M.	Lott	H	Private	Private
J.W.	Lott	F	Private	Private
James L.	Lott	H	Private	Private
Jesse Bryant	Lott	F	Private	Corporal
Jessee Benton	Lott	F	Private	Private
Kenneth M.	Lott	H	Private	Private
Nathan W.	Lott	F	Private	Private
R.C.	Lott	G	Sergeant	Sergeant
R.M.	Lott	H	Private	Private
W.M.	Lott	F	Private	Private
William A.	Lott	F	Private	Private
William J.	Lott	F	Private	Second Lieutenant
William R.	Lott	G	Private	Private
Jesse B.	Lott, Jr.	F	Private	Corporal
Jesse B.	Lott, Sr.	F	Private	Private
A.B.	Love	D	Private	Private

Ephraim O.	Lyles	K	Sergeant	Sergeant
E.W.	Lyon	H	Private	Private
Elijah W.	Lyons	H	Private	Private
Jacob	Lyons	L	Private	Sergeant
W.S.	Mabry	E	Private	Private
William	Mackey	G	Private	Private
Jesse C.	Madden	I	Corporal	First Sergeant
L.B.	Magrew	F	Private	Private
R.L.	Magrew	F	Private	Private
L.B.	Magrue	F	Private	Private
R.L.	Magrue	F	Private	Private
Patrick	Mahan	D	Private	Private
Patrick	Mahon	D	Private	Private
James M.	Major	C	Private	Second Lieutenant
David	Majors	E	Private	Private
Andrew J.	Makamson	A	Private	Private
William	Mallet	L	Private	Private
Robert J.	Mangum	D	Private	Private
F.M.	Manning	A	Private	Private
J.D.	Manning	A	Private	Private
J.W.	Manning	A	Private	Private
James Douglas	Manning	A	Private	Private
William A.	Manning	E	Private	Private
James W.	Marshall	K	Private	Sergeant
A.	Martin	G	Private	
Charles	Martin	G	Private	Private
H.A.	Martin	G	Musician	Private
J.C.	Martin	A	Private	Private
John	Martin	G	Private	Private
John W.	Martin	G	Private	Private
T.A.	Martin	E	Private	Private
John J.	Maskew	B	Corporal	Private
Byron C.	Massey	E	Private	Private
James L.	Massey	I	Private	Private
William S.	Mathews	F	Sergeant	Sergeant
James W.	Maxwell	K	Private	Private
H. Valentine	Mayfield	K	Corporal	Corporal
Robert L.	Mays	K	Private	Private
R.	McAninch	E	Private	Private
T.R.	McArmick	H	Private	Private

D.	McArthur	B	Private	Private
G.S.	McAuley	E	Private	Private
F.R.	McAunich	H	Private	Private
James	McAvoy	D	Private	Private
George C.	McCallum	G	Private	Private
Thomas	McCarbel	G	Private	Private
Thomas	McCardel	G	Private	Private
Thomas	McCardle	G	Private	Private
J.P.	McCartney	D	Private	Private
John	McCartney	D	Private	Private
Joshua S.	McCauley	E	Private	Private
Samuel G.	McCauley	E	Private	Private
James	McClearney	H	Private	Private
D.J.	McCloud	F	Second Lieutenant	First Lieutenant
George C.	McCollum	G	Private	Private
James U.	McCormick	H	Third Lieutenant	Second Lieutenant
John H.C.	McCormick	H	Private	Private
Thomas R.	McCormick	H	Private	Private
W.C.	McCormick	H	Sergeant	Sergeant
W.G.	McCormick	H	Sergeant	Sergeant
William George	McCormick	H	Sergeant	Sergeant
Duncan T.	McCraney	B,H	Private	Private
James	McCraney	H	Private	Private
Neil	McCraney	H	Private	Private
W.D.T.	McCrory	G	Private	Private
James R.	McCullough	C	Private	Private
Samuel G.	McCurley	E	Private	Private
A.	McDonald	B	Private	Sergeant
Archibald	McDonald	F	Private	First Sergeant
D.	McDonald	G	Private	Private
H.	McDonald	B	Private	Private
John W.	McDonald	H	Private	Private
Peter	McDonald	G	Private	Corporal
Duncane	McDonnel	G	Private	Private
Peter	McDonnel	G	Private	Corporal
Thomas W.	McDow	D	Private	Private
D.E.	McEachron	E	Private	Private
R.D.	McFadden	E	Private	Private
James	McGee	B	Private	Private
Daniel	McGilvery	B	Private	Private

R.L.	McGreen	F	Private	Private
R.L.	McGreer	F	Private	Private
James	McGrew	B	Private	Sergeant
James C.	McGrew	B	Private	Sergeant
L.B.	McGrew	F	Private	Private
R.L.	McGrew	F	Private	Private
William	McGrew	B	Private	Private
J.	McGrue	B	Private	Sergeant
William	McGrue	B	Private	Private
Robert	McInich	E	Private	Private
Robert	McIninch	E	Private	Private
D.S.	McInnis	G	Sergeant	Sergeant
John M.	McInnis	L	Sergeant	Second Lieutenant
Norman	McInnis	F	Private	Private
Thomas J.	McInnis	F	Private	Private
S.M.	McIntosh	E	Private	Second Lieutenant
John M.	McJames	L	Sergeant	Second Lieutenant
William	McKay	G	Private	Private
William W.	McKee	A	Private	Private
F.	McKensey	F	Private	Private
Augustus	McKenzie	F	Private	Private
F.	McKenzie	F	Private	Private
William	McKey	G	Private	Private
James B.	McKinney	K	Private	Private
Thomas B.	McKinney	K	Private	Private
Thomas M.	McKinney	D	Private	Private
W.	McKinzie	F	Private	Private
Calvin	McLaren	H	Private	Private
H.N.	McLaren	H	Private	Private
J.C.	McLaren	H	Private	Private
J.W.	McLaren	H	First Sergeant	Sergeant
Calvin	McLaurin	H	Private	Private
Hugh H.	McLaurin	H	Private	Private
Hugh N.	McLaurin	H	Private	Private
Hugh R.	McLaurin	F	Captain	Captain
J.W.	McLaurin	H	First Sergeant	Sergeant
James C.	McLaurin	H	Private	Private
W.	McLemore	B	Captain	Major
William B.	McLemore	I	Private	Private
Allen	McLeod	H	Private	Private

Azuriah R.	McLeod	F	Private	Private
Daniel Annis	McLeod	F	Second Lieutenant	First Lieutenant
Daniel J.	McLeod	F	Private	Private
Daniel J.	McLeod	F	Second Lieutenant	First Lieutenant
Kenneth A.	McLeod	L	Private	Private
Hugh M.	McLeurin	H	Private	Private
Thomas J.	McManus	F	Private	Private
William A.	McMellan	K	Sergeant	Second Lieutenant
Egbert P.	McMickle	H	Private	Private
Augustus	McMillan	K	Private	Private
N.	McMillan	E	Private	Private
William A.	McMillan	K	Sergeant	Second Lieutenant
Augustus	McMiller	K	Private	Private
W.A.	McMullen	K	Sergeant	Second Lieutenant
Jesse	McNeely	C	Sergeant	Sergeant
John W.	McNeice	F	Private	Private
R.H.	McPherson	E	Private	Private
Rufus K.	McPherson	E	Private	Private
Rufus	McPhierson	E	Private	Private
Joseph	McPhillin	E	Private	Private
J.	McPhilling	E	Private	Private
John S.	McRae	K	Private	Private
Duncan	McRaney	B,H	Private	Private
James	McRaney	H	Private	Private
Neil	McRaney	H	Private	Private
D.T.	McRany	B,H	Private	Private
John S.	McRea	K	Private	Private
William D.T.	McRory	G	Private	Private
James	McSwain	G	Private	Private
John M.	Meador	K	Private	Private
John M.	Mealer	K	Private	Private
W.	Measels	I	Private	Private
John	Meiser	E	Private	Private
Isaac W.	Merchant	E	Private	Private
James	Merchant	E	Private	Private
Robert T.	Merchant	E	Private	Private
Isaac	Merritt	G	Private	Private
S.T.	Merritt	G	Private	Private
Zachariah	Mewshaw	K	Private	Private
D.	Meyers	E	Private	Private

J.W.	Michell	C	Private	Private
James W.	Miles	E	Private	Private
John T.	Miles	E	Private	Private
W.E.	Millbanks	E	Private	Private
Frederick	Mills	I	Private	Private
J.P.	Mills	E	Private	Private
Patrick	Mills	I	Private	Private
William W.	Mills	H	Private	Private
M.A.R.	Milton	I	Private	Private
Robert A.	Minnis	K	Private	Private
Andrew J.	Mitchell	F	Private	Private
C.P.	Mitchell	F	Private	Private
G.W.	Mitchell	F	Private	Private
John F.	Mitchell	H	Corporal	Corporal
John W.	Mitchell	C	Private	Private
M.J.	Mitchell	F	Private	Private
T.J.	Mitchell	F	Private	Private
Thomas	Mitchell	F	Private	Private
Franklin J.	Mixon	G	Private	Private
James W.	Mixon	B	Private	Private
Reuben	Mixon	G	Private	Private
W.H.H.	Mixon	G	Private	Private
Luke	Mizell	L	Private	Private
Phillip	Mizell	L	Private	Private
William	Mizell	L	Private	Private
Luke	Mizzell	L	Private	Private
W.H.	Monger	H	Private	Sergeant
James M.	Montgomery	K	Private	Private
J.	Moody	I	Private	Private
Abner W.	Moore	K	Private	Private
J. D.	Moore	E	Private	Private
J. F.	Moore	I	Private	Private
James P.	Moore	H	Private	Private
Marion F.	Moore	K	Private	Private
Reubin T.	Moore	H	Private	Private
Nathaniel	Moree	F	Private	Private
George W.	Morehead		Private	Private
James D.	Morgan	K	Private	Private
Joel B.	Morgan	H	Private	Private
Joel P.	Morgan	H	Private	Private

John D.	Morgan	H	Private	Sergeant
John D.	Morgan	K	Private	Private
Vincent	Morgan	G	Private	
William G.	Morgan	H	Private	Private
William H.	Moriger	H	Private	Sergeant
Benjamin F.	Morris	H	Sergeant	Second Lieutenant
James S.	Morris	H	Private	First Sergeant
John	Morris		Private	Private
Thomas C.	Morris	H	Private	Private
Silas H.	Moseley	A	Private	Private
S. M.	Mosely	A	Private	Private
Silas M.	Mosely	A	Private	Private
S. M.	Mosley	A	Private	Private
B. C.	Mossey	E	Private	Private
William H.	Mounger	H	Private	Sergeant
James	Mowdy	I	Private	Private
Michael	Mowdy	I	Private	Private
George W.	Muirhead		Private	Private
L. A.	Mullison	E	Private	Private
W. H.	Munger	H	Private	Sergeant
W. S.	Murphey	D	Corporal	Corporal
William	Murphey	D	Corporal	Corporal
Benjamin A.	Murphy	D	Private	Private
J. F.	Murphy	A	Private	Private
J. H.	Murphy	A	Private	Private
W. S.	Murphy	D	Corporal	Corporal
David K.	Murray	L	Private	Private
George W.	Murray	L	Private	Private
Thomas J.	Murray	L	Private	Private
William	Murray	L	Private	Private
J.	Murson	E	Private	Private
George	Myers	L	Private	Private
Theodore	Myers	G	Private	
Eli	Myric	G	Private	Private
Ransey	Myric	G	Private	Private
Eli	Myrick	G	Private	Private
R.	Myrick	G	Private	Private
William	Myzell	L	Private	Private
W. M.	Nabors	C	Private	Private
William H.	Nabors	C	Private	Private

Edward D.	Nash	K	Private	Private
James M.	Nash	E	Private	Second Lieutenant
William M.	Nash	K	Private	Private
John C.	Neal	E	Private	Private
Robert	Neal	D	Corporal	Corporal
William C.	Neal	E	Private	Private
John C.	Neill	E	Private	Private
Samuel P.	Neill	E	Private	Private
William C.	Neill	E	Private	Private
E. R.	Neilson	D,B	Captain	Captain
Charles A.	Nelson	C	Private	Private
E. R.	Nelson	D,B	Captain	Captain
Ebenezer	Nelson	G	Private	Private
Joshua	Nelson	C	Private	Private
Robert	Nelson	C	Private	Private
William A.	Nelson	C	Private	Private
William M.	Nelson	C	Private	Private
J. O.	Newman	I	Private	
Richard	Newsom	B	Private	Private
Henry	Nichols	B	Private	Private
Henry W.	Nichols	B	Private	Private
Joel D.	Nichols	G	Private	Private
Joel D.	Nickland	G	Private	Private
Edward J.	Nicks	G	Private	Private
Ambrose	Nix	C	Private	Private
Edward	Nix	G	Private	Private
Goodwyn	Nixon	H	Captain	Captain
John E.	Noel	D	First Sergeant	Second Lieutenant
E.	O'Donald	E	Private	Private
John	O'Donald	E	Private	Private
Edward	O'Donell	E	Private	Private
John	O'Donnell	E	Private	Private
N. F.	O'Stein	D,B	Private	Private
Harris	Odaniel	D	Private	Private
Henry T.	Odaniel	D	Private	Private
Thomas H.	Odaniel	D	Private	Private
William	Odell	D	Private	Private
W. A.	Odenn	G	Private	Private
Albert	Odinn	G	Private	Private
Albert	Odium	G	Private	Private

W. M.	Odneer	G	Private	Private
Albert	Odom	G	Private	Private
Alson E.	Odom	G	Private	Private
Asberry	Odom	G	Private	Private
N.	Odom	G	Private	Private
William A.	Odom	G	Private	Private
A.	Odonal	E	Private	Private
Albert	Odum	G	Private	Private
W. A.	Odum	G	Private	Private
William M.	Ogborne	K	Sergeant	Sergeant
William C.	Ogle	F	Private	Private
F. M.	Osteen	D,B	Private	Private
F. M.	Osteine	D,B	Private	Private
Francis M.	Ostine	D,B	Private	Private
Soloman	Oswald	L	Private	Private
Henry	Oswalt	A	Private	Private
James W.	Oswalt	A	Private	Private
Soloman	Oswell	L	Private	Private
James	Overstreet	B	Private	Private
John	Overstreet	B	Private	Private
Benjamin	Owens	I	Private	
C. P.	Owens	E	Private	Private
Calvin R.	Owens	C	Private	Private
Francis S.	Owens	F	Private	Private
H.	Owens	F	Corporal	Corporal
William J. B.	Owens	D	Private	Private
J. D.	Page	B	Private	Private
John	Page	B	Private	Private
A. H.	Paines	B	Private	Private
G. A.	Palm	F	Private	Sergeant
J. A.	Palm	F	Private	Sergeant
A.	Palmer		Sergeant	Sergeant
William T.	Pare	C	Private	Private
William Thomas	Pare	C	Private	Private
I.	Parish	E	Private	Private
William N.	Parish	E	Private	Private
Anderson	Parker	I	Private	Private
Hubbard	Parker	L	Private	Private
John R.	Parker	G	Private	Private
Miles	Parker	H	Private	

Miles	Parker	I	Private	
S. J.	Parker	E	Private	Private
A. J.	Parrott	E	Private	Second Lieutenant
H. A.	Parrott	E	Private	Second Lieutenant
William	Passow	L	Private	Private
Jn. P.	Pate	C	Private	Private
John W.	Patison	K	Private	Private
G. W.	Patterson	D	Private	Private
George	Patterson	D	Private	Private
George W.	Patterson	F	Private	Ordnance Sergeant
J. D.	Patterson	F	Private	Corporal
John W.	Patterson	K	Private	Private
Daniel A.	Patton	F,B	Private	Sergeant
Jerry	Pearce	G	Private	Private
W. F.	Pearce	I	Private	Private
William	Pearce	G	Private	Private
James W.	Peck	K	Private	Private
Samuel M.	Pegg	B	Sergeant	Captain
Wm. A.	Pennell	B	Private	Private
A. J.	Penott	E	Private	Second Lieutenant
J.H.	Perkins	E	Private	Private
Stephen R.	Perry	G	Private	Private
W. J.	Perry	E	Private	Private
W. R.	Perry	E	Private	Private
Wm. E.	Perry	G	Private	
John	Pessaw	H,L	Private	Private
Jno. R.	Peters	K	Private	Private
Richard H.	Peters	K	Private	Private
David W.	Pettigrew	I	Private	Private
Jasper T.	Phillips	H	Second Lieutenant	Second Lieutenant
M. C.	Phillips	I	Private	Private
Benjamin F.	Pickett	L	Private	Corporal
W. F.	Pierce	I	Private	Private
S.	Pilcher	C	Private	Private
William	Pilcher	C	Private	Private
W. M.	Pinnell	B	Private	Private
William	Pinnell	B	Private	Private
J. W.	Pittman	B	Private	Private
James M.	Pittman	B	Private	Private
Joseph W.	Pittman	B	Private	Private

L. F.	Pittman	B	Private	Corporal
W. T.	Pittman	B	Private	Private
Benjamin	Pitts	G	Private	Private
G. W.	Pitts	G	Private	Private
Henry	Pitts	G	Private	Private
James	Pitts	G	Private	Private
James E.	Pitts	B	Private	Private
Jesse	Pitts	G	Private	Private
Joshua	Pitts	G	Private	Private
Nehemiah	Pitts	G	Private	Private
William F.	Polk	G	Private	Private
John R.	Poole	C	Private	Captain
J. T.	Pope	E	Private	Private
Joel	Pope	E	Private	Private
Fred S.	Porter	K	Private	Private
Theodrick S.	Porter	K	Private	Private
T. S.	Potter	K	Private	Private
Anderson G.	Powell	K	Private	Sergeant
James	Powell	B	Private	Private
Robert H.	Powell	F	Private	Private
M. P.	Powers	G	Private	First Sergeant
Isaac	Prescott	B	Private	Private
J.	Prescott	B	Private	Private
Thomas H.	Presley	E	Private	Private
W.T.	Price	D	Private	Private
Richard	Prichett	H		
S.C.	Pride	H	Private	Private
E.H.	Prince	D	Private	Private
Loverick W.	Prince	D	Private	Private
William L.	Prince	D	Private	Corporal
Joseph	Prine	H	Private	Private
L.C.	Prine	H	Private	Private
S.C.	Prine	H	Private	Private
Silas C.	Prine	H	Private	Private
William H.	Prine	B	Private	Private
Joseph W.	Pruitt	A	Private	Private
Allen C.	Puckett	K	Private	Private
William H.	Puckett	K	Private	Private
Joseph P.	Pulliam	K	Private	Private
Nathan F.	Pullin	K	Private	Private

Thomas	Quack	B	Private	Private
F.	Quarles	D	Private	Private
James L.	Quarles	D	Private	Private
Lafayette	Quarles	D	Private	Private
Thomas C.	Quick	B	Private	Private
William	Quick	B	Private	Private
James	Quinn	E	Private	Private
F.M.	Rabjohn	D	Private	Private
Stephen	Rabjohn	D	Private	Private
F.M.	Rainey	E	Private	Private
O.C.	Rainey	G	Private	Private
A.H.	Rains	B	Private	Private
William	Rainwater	B	Private	Sergeant
William F.	Ramsay	I	Private	Private
William T.	Ramsey	I	Private	Private
William T.	Ramsie	I	Private	Private
William T.	Ramsle	I	Private	Private
W.F.	Ramzey	I	Private	Private
Thomas C.	Rasberry	E	Private	Private
Thomas C.	Raspberry	E	Private	Private
Elisha P.	Ratcliff	B	Private	Private
F.	Rathio	E	Private	Private
E.P.	Ratliff	B	Private	Private
Felix S.	Rawles	B	Private	Sergeant
J.T.	Rawles	B	Private	Sergeant
A.J.	Ray	A	Private	Private
Andrew J.	Ray	C	Private	Private
Franklin A.	Ray	C	Private	Private
William M.	Ray	I	Private	Private
William	Read	E	Private	Private
C.	Reaves	G	Private	Private
A.J.	Reck	H	Private	Private
L.	Redding	C	Private	Private
J.R.	Reed	H	Private	Private
Joseph	Reed	L	Private	Private
Edward D.	Reel	A	Private	Private
Jack	Reel	A	Private	Musician
John	Reel	A	Private	Musician
M.W.	Reeves	I	Private	
Oliver C.	Reeves	G	Private	Private

Oscar C.	Reeves	G	Private	Private
Thomas	Reeves	G	Private	Private
William	Reeves	H	Private	Private
William	Reevies	H	Private	Private
James R.	Reid	H	Private	Private
Jesse B.	Reid	F	Private	Private
J.	Rell	A	Private	Musician
J.H.	Renolds	B	Private	Private
J.	Reynolds	L	Private	Private
James H.	Reynolds	B	Private	Private
Joseph H.	Reynolds	C	Private	Private
William G.	Reynolds	B	Private	Corporal
Andrew J.	Rhea	C	Private	Private
Francis A.	Rhea	C	Private	Private
George W.	Rice	D	Private	Private
Joel D.	Rice	D	Private	Private
A.J.	Rich	H	Private	Private
Richard G.	Richler	L	Sergeant	Sergeant
A.J.	Rick	H	Private	Private
Richard G.	Rictor	L	Sergeant	Sergeant
Richard G.	Rider	L	Sergeant	Sergeant
James R.	Riggs	G	Private	Sergeant
Asa W.	Risher	H	Private	Private
Christopher C.	Risher	H	Private	Private
James W.	Risher	H	Private	Private
Whitelock	Risher	H	Private	Private
William	Risher	H	Private	Private
Elisha F.	Rivers	C	Private	Second Lieutenant
R.C.	Rivers	C	Private	Private
G.W.	Roberson	C	Private	Private
J.D.	Roberson	C	Private	Sergeant
J.W.	Roberson	B	Private	Private
James M.	Roberson	E	Private	Private
William	Roberson	E	Private	Private
William H.	Roberson	F	Private	Private
Adoniram J.	Robertson	F	Private	Corporal
Benjamin F.	Robertson	F	Private	Private
C.H.	Robertson	A	Sergeant	Sergeant
George W.	Robertson	F	Private	Private
John T.	Robertson	A	Private	Private

Stephen	Robertson	A	Private	Private
Thomas	Robertson	A	Private	Private
W.C.	Robertson	A	Private	Private
William	Robins	C	Private	Private
B.W.	Robinson	C	Private	Private
G.W.	Robinson	F	Private	Private
J.L.	Robinson	C	Private	Sergeant
J.M.	Robinson	E	Private	Private
J.R.	Robinson	H	Corporal	Private
James D.	Robinson	C	Private	Sergeant
John T.	Robinson	A	Private	Private
John W.	Robinson	I	Private	Private
Joseph	Robinson	H	Corporal	Private
W.B.	Robinson	C	Private	Private
W.C.	Robinson	A	Private	Private
William	Robinson	E	Private	Private
J.W.	Robison	B	Private	Private
Burrell	Rodgers	H	Private	Private
Burwell	Rodgers	H	Private	Private
David C.	Rodgers	F	Private	Private
Edwin A.	Rodgers	K	Private	Private
John A.	Rodgers	H	Private	Private
Mike	Rodgers	H	Private	First Lieutenant
Oscar	Rodgers	K	Private	Private
S.C.	Rodgers	F	Private	Private
Burwell	Rogers	H	Private	Private
D.C.	Rogers	F	Private	Private
Edwin A.	Rogers	K	Private	Private
F.M.	Rogers	B	Private	Private
Levy C. Lee	Rogers	F	Private	Private
Mike	Rogers	H	Private	First Lieutenant
Oscar	Rogers	K	Private	Private
R.J.	Rogers	E	Private	Private
William G.	Rogers	B	Private	Private
William Jasper	Rogers	B	Private	Private
Griffin	Ross	D	Private	Private
M.E.	Ross	D	Private	Private
Martin	Ross	D	Private	Private
Richard P.	Ross	D	Private	Private
Frank	Rotton	E	Private	Private

Abraham J.	Rowell	H	Private	Private
D.J.	Rowell	H	Private	Private
David H.	Rowell	H	Private	Private
Elihu	Rowell	H	Private	Private
Eliphus	Rowell	H	Private	Private
I.B.	Rowell	H		
J.A.	Rowell	H	Private	Private
J.D.	Rowell	H	Private	Private
James D.	Rowell	H	Private	Private
S.	Rowell	H	Private	
W.B.	Rowell	H	Private	Private
W.W.	Rozel	A	Private	Private
J.W.	Rush	B	Private	Private
I.H.	Rushing	E	Private	Private
N.R.	Rushing	E	Private	Private
Richard G.	Ryder	L	Sergeant	Sergeant
John B.	Sale	K	Captain	Captain
William H.	Salisbury	L	Private	Private
William H.	Salsbury	L	Private	Private
Daniel	Sanders	E	Private	Private
H.H.	Sanders	C	Private	Private
J.W.	Sanders	A	Private	Private
T.J.D.	Sanders	E	Private	Corporal
Thomas J.	Sanders	E	Private	Corporal
W.H.	Sanders	K	Second Lieutenant	First Lieutenant
W.J.	Sanders	E	Private	Private
E.	Sanderson	B	Private	Private
J.H.	Sanderson	B	Sergeant	Sergeant
Nicholas H.	Sannichson	L	Private	Private
James H.	Sansing	A	Private	Private
M.A.	Sansing	A	Private	Private
Martin	Sansing	A	Private	Private
W. H.	Saulsbury	L	Private	Private
F. M.	Saunders	A	Private	
H. H.	Saunders	C	Private	Private
William H.	Saunders	K	Second Lieutenant	First Lieutenant
J.	Sausing	A	Private	Private
Zachariah T.	Savage	K	Private	Private
Nicholas H.	Scanichson	L	Private	Private
R. W.	Scarbar	H	Private	Private

W. R.	Scarber	H	Private	Private
Wiley J.	Scarber	F	Private	Private
Wiley J.	Scarborough	F	Private	Private
William R.	Scarborough	H	Private	Private
William	Scarbrough	H	Private	Private
David S.	Scerteries	C	Corporal	First Sergeant
G. W.	Scott	F	Sergeant	Sergeant
Benjamin F.	Scovell	L	Private	Private
Joseph	Scruggs	H	Private	Private
R. J.	Scruggs	H	Private	Private
William	Seales	E	Private	Private
Hardy	Sellars	B	Private	Private
John A.	Sellars	B	Private	Private
J. W.	Scllers	B	Privatc	Private
Benjamin	Serlay	H	Private	Private
T.	Sewall	I	Private	Private
E. S.	Seward	I	Private	Private
James H.	Sexton	C	Private	Private
S.	Seymore	F	Private	Private
John	Shack	E	Private	Private
Allen	Shader	E	Private	Private
Marion	Shader	E	Private	Private
George S.	Shearer	E	Private	Private
John W.	Shearley	B	Private	Corporal
E. R.	Sheeley	D	Private	Private
William W.	Sheeley	D	Private	Private
I. A.	Shelby	E	Private	Private
Jn. S.	Sheldon	D	Private	Sergeant
John S.	Sheldon	D	Private	Sergeant
J. A.	Shelly	F&S	Assistant Surgeon	Assistant Surgeon
Columbus L.	Shelton	C	Private	Private
Elijah H.	Shelton	C	Private	Private
James V.	Shelton	C	Private	Private
John S.	Shelton	D	Private	Sergeant
John W.	Shelton	C	Private	Private
Samuel W.	Shelton	C	Private	Private
Vincent H.	Shelton	C	Private	Private
W. R.	Shen	D	Private	Private
William	Shepard	E	Private	Private
W. M.	Shepherd	E	Private	Private

William	Shepherd	E	Private	Private
George S.	Sherar	E	Private	Private
R. M.	Sherd	F	Private	Private
R. W.	Sherd	F	Private	Private
George S.	Sherer	E	Private	Private
Benjamin	Sherley	H	Private	Private
J. W.	Sherley	B	Private	Corporal
Walter	Sherman	D	Private	Private
R. W.	Sherod	F	Private	Private
Samuel	Sherrell	D	Private	Private
Samuel B.	Sherrill	D	Private	Private
Samuel Pinckney	Sherrill	D	Private	Private
Robert	Sherrod	F	Private	Private
W. R.	Shew	D	Private	Private
A. W.	Shirley	B	Private	Corporal
Benjamin	Shirley	H	Private	Private
J. W.	Shirley	B	Private	Corporal
J. W.	Shirley	B	Private	Corporal
Benjamin	Shirly	H	Private	Private
Thomas	Shivers	F	Private	Private
William	Shivers	F	Private	Private
B. H.	Sholar	G	Private	Private
A. B.	Short	F	Private	Private
John	Shuck	E	Private	Private
William R.	Shue	D	Private	Private
John W.	Simmonds	E	Private	Private
William	Simmonds	E	Private	Corporal
Benjamin D.	Simmons	A	Corporal	Sergeant
Benjamin F.	Simmons	G	Private	Private
Isaiah	Simmons	L	Private	Private
James	Simmons	L	Private	Private
John	Simmons	L	Drummer	Drummer
John W.	Simmons	E	Private	Private
William S.	Simmons	E	Private	Corporal
L.	Simms	A	Corporal	Sergeant
B.D.	Simons	A	Corporal	Sergeant
Benjamin D.	Sims	A	Corporal	Sergeant
Benjamin D.	Sins	A	Corporal	Sergeant
B.W.	Sintzell	C	Private	Private
J.W.	Sirley	B	Private	Corporal

James R.	Sively	K	Private	Private
Alexander J.	Smith	B	Private	Private
Benjamin F.	Smith	I	Private	
D.A.	Smith	B	Private	Private
D.C.	Smith	B	Private	Private
Daniel	Smith	B	Musician	Musician
Daniel	Smith	B	Private	Private
Daniel W.	Smith	C	Private	Private
Duncan P.	Smith	B	Private	Sergeant
George T.	Smith	C	First Sergeant	Third Lieutenant
George W.	Smith	K	Private	Private
Harry H.	Smith	F	Private	Private
J.A.	Smith	B	Private	Private
J.B.	Smith	F	Private	Private
J.M.	Smith	E	Private	Private
J.M.	Smith	F	Private	Private
J.R.	Smith	A	Private	Private
James	Smith	E	Private	Private
James A.	Smith	B	Private	Private
James M.	Smith	K	Private	Private
John	Smith	L	Private	Private
John M.	Smith	E	Private	Private
John R.	Smith	D	Private	Private
Julian E.	Smith	K	Private	Private
L.J.	Smith	B	Private	Private
Leroy	Smith	G	Private	Private
Levi	Smith	L	Private	Private
Levi S.	Smith	L	Private	Private
Malcom W.	Smith	F	Private	Sergeant
N.W.	Smith	F	Private	Sergeant
Neil C.	Smith	F	Private	Private
Owen	Smith	D	Private	Private
Simeon H.	Smith	B	Brevet Second Lieutenant	First Lieutenant
Stanford	Smith	D	Private	Private
T.M.	Smith	A	Private	Private
Thomas B.	Smith	K	First Sergeant	First Sergeant
W.C.	Smith	I	Private	Private
Wilford C.	Smith	D	Private	Private
William	Smith	B	Musician	Private

William A.	Smith	F	Private	Private
William J.	Smith	C	Private	Private
William M.	Smith	C	Private	Private
George W.	Smithin	D	Private	Private
M.M.	Snead	C	Private	Private
M.W.	Snead	C	Private	Private
Asa L.	Sneed	C	Private	Private
Asa M.	Sneed	C	Private	Private
L.	Sneed	B	Private	Private
Maston M.	Sneed	C	Private	Private
Melcijah M.	Sneed	C	Private	Private
Thomas	Snider	E	Private	Private
W.C.	Snow	A	Private	Private
Augustus V.	Snowden	K	Third Lieutenant	Junior Second Lieutenant
William C.	Snown	A	Private	Private
Benjamin	Socovell	L	Private	Private
Smith	Somers	I	Private	Private
N.H.	Sonnichsen	L	Private	Private
Allen	Spader	E	Private	Private
Marion	Spader	E	Private	Private
Marvin	Spader	E	Private	Private
Citizen	Sparks	C	Private	Private
Marion	Speight	E	Private	Private
Allen	Speights	E	Private	Private
James A.	Speights	E	Private	Private
William M.	Speights	E	Private	Private
J.A.	Speits	E	Private	Private
George H.	Speller	F	Private	Sergeant
J.A.	Spights	E	Private	Private
George W.	Spillers	F	Private	Sergeant
Herschell D.	Spratt	K	Private	
A.	Sprights	E	Private	Private
Edward W.	Stafford	H	First Lieutenant	Captain
W.S.	Stafford	H	First Lieutenant	Captain
Isaac B.	Stanton	A	Private	Sergeant
J.V.	Stanton	A	Private	Sergeant
Joseph M.	Steel	A	Private	Private
Peter	Stemitz	E	Private	Private
William	Stephens	G	Sergeant	Sergeant

Wilson M.	Stephens	H	Private	Private
Wm. M.	Stephens	N	Private	Private
William	Stevens	G	Sergeant	Sergeant
T.A.	Steward	B	Private	Private
John C.	Stewart	F	Corporal	Private
T.A.	Stewart	B	Private	Private
William E.	Stewart	B	Private	Corporal
Henry	Sticker	L	Private	Private
Nicholas	Sticker	L	Private	Private
Henry	Stickler	L	Private	Private
Hen	Sticklin	G	Private	Private
P.B.	Stinson	G	Private	Private
Joel	Stokes	B	Private	Private
John F.	Stone	D	Private	Private
John T.	Stone	D	Private	Private
Green W.	Strawn	C	Private	Private
W.G.	Strawn	C	Private	Private
Daniel M.	Strickland	F	Private	Private
Henry	Strickland	G	Private	Private
Henry	Stricklin	G	Private	Private
S.P.	Strill	E	Private	Private
Thomas J.	Strong	C	Private	Private
William	Strong	L	Private	Private
William G.	Stroun	C	Private	Private
T.A.	Stuart	B	Private	Private
W.E.	Stuart	B	Private	Corporal
Jesse	Sulivan	D	Private	Private
Jessee	Sullavant	D	Private	Private
Jessee	Sullivant	D	Private	Private
Silas	Sullivant	D	Private	Private
Jessee	Sullivant, Jun.	D	Private	Private
Silas	Sulliwant	D	Private	Private
Hiram A.	Summers	D	Sergeant	Sergeant
S.S.	Summers	I	Private	Private
Smith	Summers, Jr.	I	Private	Private
S.	Sumner	I	Private	Private
H.A.	Sumners	D	Sergeant	Sergeant
Charles R.	Sumrall	L	Private	Private
J.W.	Sumrall	G	Private	Private
Levi	Sumrall	G	Private	Private

James W.	Suttle	E	Private	Private
Joseph W.	Suttle	E	Private	Private
Benjamin W.	Switzer	C	Private	Private
David S.	Switzer	C	Corporal	First Sergeant
Samuel J.	Switzer	C	Corporal	First Sergeant
Albert G.	Swor	F	Private	Sergeant
J.H.	Tait	D	Private	Private
B.A.	Tardy	C	First Lieutenant	First Lieutenant
Thomas H.	Tardy	C	Private	Private
T.E.	Tatam	G	Private	Private
John P.	Tate	C	Private	Private
T.E.	Tatum	G	Private	Private
A.A.	Taylor	E	Private	Private
B.	Taylor	F	Private	Private
B.F.	Taylor	E	Private	Musician
Francis B.	Taylor	E	Private	Musician
Jesse	Taylor	G	Private	Private
John W.	Taylor	C	Private	Private
Perry J.	Taylor	C	Private	Private
Wallace	Taylor	D	Private	Private
Walter	Taylor	D	Private	Private
Wiley W.	Taylor	C	Private	Private
William W.	Taylor	C	Private	Private
Joshua	Terral	H	Private	Private
W.F.	Terral	H	Private	Private
J.S.	Terrell	H	Third Lieutenant	Third Lieutenant
Joshua	Terrell	H	Private	Private
William	Thames	F	Private	Private
Andrew J.	Thomas	G	Private	Sergeant
Leander A.	Thomas	E	Private	Private
Lee	Thomas	E	Private	Private
William	Thomas	F	Private	Private
William W.	Thomas	G	Private	Private
D.W.	Thompson	A	Private	Private
J.H.	Thompson	A	Private	Private
James S.	Thompson	K	Private	Private
Jeremiah	Thompson	A	Private	Private
Jerry	Thompson	A	Private	Private
Jesse G.	Thompson	L	Sergeant	Second Lieutenant
John M.	Thompson	G	Sergeant	Third Lieutenant

Joseph H.	Thompson	K	Private	Private
Joseph U.	Thompson	L	Private	Private
Lewis W.	Thompson	L	Private	Private
O.C.	Thompson	H	Musician	Private
Samuel E.	Thompson	K	Private	Private
Simon	Thompson	L	Private	Private
James	Thrailkill	K	Private	Private
William	Thrasher	I	Private	Private
William	Thrasker	I	Private	Private
David	Threhern	L	Private	Private
James	Threlkeld	K	Private	Private
R.G.	Thweatt	E	Private	Private
J.L.	Tippett	B	Private	Private
James L.	Tippit	B	Private	Private
W.J.	Tippit	B	Private	Private
Isaac D.	Tisdale	G	Private	Private
S.	Tisdale	G	Private	Private
A.R.	Tourner	E	Private	Private
John A.	Towner	E	Private	Private
John B.	Townsend	K	Private	Private
Thomas B.	Townsend	K	Private	Private
J.B.	Townson	K	Private	Private
David	Trahern	L	Private	Private
James	Trailkill	K	Private	Private
Ezechial S.	Travis	G	Private	Private
John A.	Travis	H	Private	Private
Loama	Travis	H	Private	Private
Lomia	Travis	H	Private	Private
W.G.	Travis	G	Private	Private
Isaac	Treadwell	E	Private	Private
W.J.	Treadwell	E	Private	Private
James	Treble	D	Private	Sergeant
David	Trehern	L	Private	Private
James M.	Tribble	D	Private	Sergeant
W.H.	Triplett	E	Private	Private
George A.	Tripp	E	Private	Private
Andrew J.	Trippe	E	Private	Private
George E.	Trippe	E	Private	Private
John G.	Truland	K	Private	Private
Benjamin F.	Tubb	K	Private	Private

Joseph W.	Tucker	H	Private	Private
A.R.	Turner	E	Private	Private
Richard A.	Turner	E	Private	Private
William M.	Turner	F	Private	Corporal
William S.	Turner	C	Private	Private
Thomas T.	Urey	E	Private	Private
T.T.	Ury	E	Private	Private
A.J.	Valentine	B	Private	Private
R.H.	Valentine	B	Private	Private
W.T.	Valentine	B	Private	Private
Andrew A.	Vaughan	L	Corporal	Corporal
Andrew A.	Vaughn	L	Corporal	Corporal
R.N.	Venable	F&S	Assistant Surgeon	Assistant Surgeon
J.N.	Vickery	B	Private	Private
Thomas L.	Vincent	L	Private	Private
Thomas	Vinson	L	Private	Private
Thompson	Vinson	L	Private	Private
Andrew J.	Volentine	B	Private	Private
R.H.	Volentine	B	Private	Private
William T.	Volentine	B	Private	Private
Andrew A.	Voyne	L	Corporal	Corporal
W.W.	Wadkins	E	Private	Private
Wm. W.	Wadkins	E	Private	Private
B.J.	Waganer	E	Private	Private
A.J.	Waggoner	E	Private	Private
B.J.	Waggoner	E	Private	Private
B.J.	Wagoner	E	Private	Private
F.M.	Waiters	H	Private	Private
Francis M.	Waits	H	Private	Private
A.C.	Walker	E	Private	Private
John	Walker	F	Private	Private
William F.	Walker	I,K	Private	Corporal
William Henry	Walker	F	Private	Private
William L.	Walker	D	Sergeant	Sergeant
Willis L.	Walker	D	Sergeant	Sergeant
B.	Wallace	C	Private	Private
Goolsberry	Walley	G	Private	Private
James	Walley	G	Private	Private
Pinkney	Walley	G	Private	Private
Thomas	Walley	G	Private	Private

Brison	Wallis	C	Private	Private
R.H.	Walter	E	Private	Private
R.H.	Waltern	E	Private	Private
J.W.	Walters	B	Private	Private
John	Walters	B	Private	Private
Joseph	Walters	L	Private	Private
Samuel	Walters	L	Private	Private
Simmeon L.	Walters	D	Private	Sergeant
R.H.	Walton	E	Private	Private
David T.	Ward	D	Private	Private
Thos. D.	Ward	D	Private	Private
W.H.	Ward	E	Second Lieutenant	
Milton	Ware	L	Private	Private
Nicholas O.	Ware	K	Private	Private
W.W.	Ware	L	Private	Private
Able	Warner	D	Private	Private
Abram B.	Warner	D	Private	Private
George O.	Warner	K	Private	Private
Arthur	Warren	C	Private	Private
Joseph	Warren	C	Private	Private
Richard	Warren	C	Private	Private
William	Warren	C	Private	Sergeant
George W.	Warrick	I	Private	Sergeant
John	Warrick	I	Private	Private
James W.	Warrington	C	Private	Private
R.	Wasser	C	Private	Private
J.E.	Waters	A	Private	Private
Thomas	Waters	A	Private	Private
Charles	Watkins	E	Private	Private
H.I.	Watkins	F&S	Private	Sergeant Major
Judson	Watkins	I	Private	Private
S.C.	Watkins	E	Private	Private
William	Watkins	E	Private	Private
Azariah W.	Watson	K	Private	Private
J.C.	Watson	A	Private	Private
Perry M.	Watson	K	Private	Private
Samuel	Watters	L	Private	Private
E.	Watts	B	Private	Sergeant
George	Watts	F	Private	Private
George M.D.	Watts	B	Private	Private

John	Watts	B	Private	Private
Martin Van Buren	Watts	F	Private	Private
R.W.	Watts	F	Private	Private
V.B.	Watts	F	Private	Private
John	Weakley	K	Private	Private
William M.	Weatherall	C	Private	Musician
Abram S.	Weatherford	I	Private	
Levi L.	Weatherford	I	Private	Private
James	Weeks	A	Private	Private
Stephen H.	Weeks	H	Private	Private
J.E.	Welborn	B	First Lieutenant	First Lieutenant
James	Welch	F	Private	Private
John	Welch	F	Private	Private
Samuel	Welch	F	Private	Private
William	Welch	L	Orderly Sergeant	Second Lieutenant
James W.	Welday	G	Private	Private
P.M.	Welday	G	Private	Private
Thomas	Welday	G	Private	Private
J.W.	Weldy	G	Private	Private
Lewis	Well	L	Private	Private
W.C.	Wellbanks	E	Private	Private
R.M.	Wellday	G	Private	Private
John J.	Wells	E	Private	Private
John J.	Wells	L	Sergeant	Private
Jordan I.	Wells	E	Private	Private
Louis	Wells	L	Private	Private
Edgar A.	West	E	Private	Private
James C.	West	B	Private	Private
Thomas W.	West	B	Private	Corporal
W.	West	E	Private	Private
John A.	Westbrook	K	Private	Private
William G.	Westbrook	K	Private	Private
William N.	Westbrook	K	Private	Private
William G.	Westbrooks	K	Private	Private
O.H.	Westlake	D	Private	Private
B.B.	Weston	A	Private	Private
Levi L.	Wetherford	I	Private	Private
John	Whateley	K	Private	Private
Wilson	Whateley	K	Private	Private
John	Whatley	K	Private	Private

Wilson	Whatley, Jr.	K	Private	Private
Ezekiel	Wheatly	C	Private	Private
Christopher R.	Wheeler	G	Private	Corporal
Erastus W.	Wheeler	H	Private	Private
John A.	Wheeler	H	Private	Private
W.	Wheeler	H	Private	Private
Hiram L.	White	K	Private	Private
Hundley V.	White	K	Private	Private
Hunley V.	White	K	Private	Private
James H.	White	K	Private	Private
James M.	White	K	Private	Private
James M.	White	K	Private	Private
James N.	White	K	Private	Private
James U.	White	K	Private	Private
James W.	White	K	Private	Private
L.M.	White	I	Private	Private
W.	White	K	Private	Private
William S.	White	I	Private	Private
D.W.	Whitehead	F	Private	Private
G.C.	Whitehead	F	Private	Private
Matthew R.	Whitehead	F	Private	Private
N.V.	Whitehead	F	Private	Private
Jesse F.	Whitley	K	Private	Private
Robert H.	Whitley	K	Private	Private
Elijah F.	Whitten	C	Private	Private
Mike C.	Whittle	H	Private	Private
Francis	Whitton	C	Private	Private
William E.	Wilbanks	E	Private	Private
William J.	Wiley	C	Second Lieutenant	First Lieutenant
William P.	Wiley	A	Private	Private
Absalom	Willaford	D	Private	Private
Absalom L.	Willanford	D	Private	Private
William	Willbanks	E	Private	Private
Absalom F.	Willeford	D	Private	Private
Elijah	Williams	C	Private	Private
Emmet	Williams	K	Private	Private
George	Williams	L	Private	Private
George W.	Williams	E	Private	Private
H.	Williams	B	Private	Private
H.C.	Williams	E	Private	Private

J.B.	Williams	D	Private	Private
James	Williams	L	Private	Private
John	Williams	E	Private	Private
John B.	Williams	L	Private	Private
Joseph	Williams	L	Private	Private
R.A.J.	Williams	E	Private	Private
S.L.	Williams	D	Private	Private
Solomon	Williams	D	Private	Private
William J.	Williams	H	Private	Private
A.L.	Williamson	F	Private	Private
Albert	Williamson	F	Private	Private
Frank	Williamson	F	Corporal	Corporal
J.P.	Williamson	F	Sergeant	Sergeant
James	Williamson	F	Private	Private
P.D.	Williamson	K	Corporal	Sergeant
Thomas D.	Williamson	K	Corporal	Sergeant
Wiley W.	Williamson	F	Private	Private
William J.	Williamson	F	Private	Private
Absolem	Williford	D	Private	Private
Daniel W.	Willis	K	Private	Private
J.	Willoughby	K	Private	Private
Seaborn J.	Willoughby	K	Private	Private
A.G.	Wilson	F	Corporal	Corporal
G.A.	Wilson	F	Corporal	Corporal
Hiram H.	Wilson	F	Private	Sergeant
S.D.	Wilson	F	Corporal	Corporal
J.L.	Winden	H	Private	Private
J.L.	Windern	H	Private	Private
James M.	Windham	H	Private	Private
James L.	Winton	H	Private	Private
William F.	Woffon	I,K	Private	Corporal
Robert H.	Wofford	K	Private	Private
William F.	Wofford	K,I	Private	Corporal
Willis F.	Wolford	I,K	Private	Corporal
A.J.	Wolverton	I	Corporal	Private
J.A.	Wood	C	Private	Private
John H.	Wood	I	Sergeant	Captain
Andrew J.	Woodall	A	Private	Private
F.M.	Woodall	A	Private	Private
James M.	Woodall	A	Private	Private

James H.	Woodard	C	Private	Private
Osborn E.	Woodard	H	Private	Private
James W.	Woodman	C	Private	Private
William M.	Woods	I	Private	Private
S.L.	Woodson	A	Corporal	Corporal
T.L.	Woodson	A	Corporal	Corporal
Ausburn E.	Woodward	H	Private	Private
James W.	Woodward	C	Private	Private
P.E.	Woodward	H	Private	Private
J.R.	Worrell	A	Private	Private
George W.	Worrick	I	Private	Sergeant
John	Worrick	I	Private	Private
Assa	Worthey	C	Private	Private
W.P.	Wyley	A	Private	Private
W.P.	Wylie	A	Private	Private
Eli	Wyrick	G	Private	Private
Jackson	Yates	F	Private	Private
Peter	Yates	B	Private	Private
Greenberry	Yawn	F	Private	Private
Joseph	Yawn	F	Private	Private
E.H.	Yelverton	L	Private	Private
Everard H.	Yelverton	L	Private	Private
J.	Yohn	G	Private	Private
John	Youhn	G	Private	Private
F.R.	Young	E	Private	Private
Franklin	Young	E	Private	Private
H.D.	Young	E	Private	Private
J.A.	Young	K	Private	Private
Robert H.	Young	E	Private	Private

*   *   *

REUNION

of the

Twenty-Seventh Mississippi Infantry Regiment

and

Companies

On Saturday, May 3rd, 1890 at 12 O'clock p.m. the survivors of the 27th Mississippi Infantry Regiment and Companies reassembled at the W. A. Mc Millan & Son's, Aberdeen, Mississippi for a grand reunion.

The keynote speaker was General Walthall.

Among the attending veterans was 2nd Lieutenant Robert Amos Jarman, Company K.

The conclusion, assembly presented General Walthall with a memento of the Battle of Chickamauga! The memento consisted of a tree root saved from the battle line filled with canister and shot from the battle and represented the critical moment in which the General rallied his brigade in a turning point action and saved the day for the units his Brigade.

General Footnotes

Chapter I-XVI.

1. Complied Service Records of Confederate Soldiers Who Served in Organizations from the State of Mississippi; National Archives Microfilm Pubs, Microcopy 269, Roll 326; National Archives and Records Service, GSA, Washington, DC; 1959

2. Sifakis, Stewart; Compendium of the Confederate Armies: Mississippi; Facts on File, Inc., New York, NY; 1995.

3. Jarman, Robert Amos; The History of Company K, 27th Mississippi Infantry, and its first and last Muster Rolls; The Aberdeen Examiner, Aberdeen, MS; 1890.

4. Rowland, Dunbar; Military History of Mississippi 1803-1898; Chickasaw Bayou Press, Madison, MS; 2003.

5. Confederate Military History: North Carolina, 12 Volumes; Confederate Publishing Co., Atlanta, GA; 1899; Volume 4.

6. McMurry, Robert M., Editor; Jarman, Robert A.; "A Mississippian at Nashville" (a soldier's view); Civil War Times Magazine, May 1973, pages 8-15.

7. Confederate Mississippi Troops: 27th Regiment Mississippi Infantry; Civil War Database, National Parks Service, National Archives and Records Center, GSA, Washington, DC, 2006.

Battle Maps and Confederate Order of Battle Tables:

8. Bush, Bryan S.; The Civil War of the Western Theater; Turner Publishing Co., Paducah, KY, 1998.

MAP LISTS

M-1. State of Mississippi, 1860
(Buttersworth, J.K.; Mississippi in the Confederacy, 1961)

M-2. Central Kentucky-Tennessee, 1862

M-3. Perryville, Kentucky 1862

M-4. Murfreesboro, Tennessee 1862-1863

M-5. North Central Georgia, 1863

M-6. Walker County, Georgia 1863

M-7. Chattanooga, Tennessee 1863

M-8. Central Georgia and Atlanta, 1864

M-9. South Atlanta and Jonesboro, Georgia 1864

M-10. Williamson County and Franklin, Tennessee 1865

M-11. Davidson County and Nashville, Tennessee 1865

M-12. Bentonville, North Carolina 1865

M-13. The Railroads of the Confederate States, 1861
(Wiley, Bell I.; The Embattled Confederates; 1964)

TABLE LISTS

ORDER OF BATTLE CONFEDERATE FORCES

1. Central Kentucky Campaign—Battle of Perryville

2. Middle Tennessee Campaign—Battle of Murfreesboro

3. Northern Georgia Campaign—Battle of Chickamauga

4. Northern Georgia Campaign—Battle of Lookout Mountain
And Missionary Ridge

5. Central Georgia Campaign—Battle of Atlanta

6. Central Tennessee Campaign—Battle of Franklin/Nashville

7. Carolina Campaign—Battle of Bentonville

8. Carolina Campaign—Final Re-Organization
(Army of Tennessee) Raleigh, N.C.

BIBLIOGRAPHY

A

B

Boatner, Mark M.; The Civil War Dictionary; David McKay Co. Inc.(Van Press Press), New York, NY; 1959.

Bush, Bryan S.; The Civil War of the Western Theater; Turner Publishing Co., Paducah, KY; 1998.

Butterworth, J.K.; Mississippi in the Confederacy, Volume 1, Louisiana State University Press, LA; 1961.

C

Complied Service Records of Confederate Soldiers Who Served in Organizations from the State of Mississippi; National Archives Microfilm Pubs, Microcopy 269, Roll 326; National Archives and Records Service, GSA; Washington, DC; 1959.

Confederate Military History, North Carolina; 12 Volume; Confederate Publishing Co., Atlanta, GA; 1899; Volume 4.

Confederate Mississippi Troops—27th Regiment Mississippi Infantry; National Archives and Records Center, National Parks Service, Civil War Database; Washington, DC; 2006.

Confederate Veteran. Hoffman, John. The Confederate Collapse at the Battle of Missionary Ridge: The Report of James Patton Anderson and his brigade commanders. Dayton, OH, 1985.

Cozzens, Peter; This Terrible Sound: the Battle of Chickamauga; University of Illinois Press, Chicago, IL; 1992.

D

E

F

Flato, Charles; The Golden Book of the Civil War; Golden Press, NY; 1961.

G

Greenwell, Dale; The Third Mississippi Regiment—C.S.A.; Lewis Printing Service;Pascagoula, MS; 1972.

H

Horn, Stanley F.; The Army of Tennessee; Babb's and Merrill Co.; NY; 1941.

Hughes, Nathaniel L.; Bentonville (The Final Battle), University of North Carolina Press, Chapel Hill, NC; 1966.

I

Illustrated Atlas of the Civil War, Time-Life Book; Alexandra, VA; 1996.

J

Jarman, R.A.; The History of Company K, 27th Mississippi Infantry, and its first and last Muster Rolls; The Aberdeen Examiner, Aberdeen, MS; 1890.

K

L

Lee, Fitzhugh; Confederate Soldier in the Civil War; The Fairfax Press (Crown Publishers), VA; 1895.

M

Mississippi Military Organizations serving in the Civil War; University of Southern Mississippi, Hattiesburg, MS; Undated.

Mc Murray, Richard M, Editor; Jarman, Robert A; "A Mississippian at Nashville" (A Soldier's View)," Civil War Times Magazine, May 1973, P. 8-15.

N

O

Office of the Adjutant General, State of Mississippi; Register of Commissions, Jackson, MS; 1861-1865.

P

Q

R

Rietti, J.C.; Military Annals of the Confederate Mississippi; Reprint Company Publishers, Spartanburg, SC; 1976.

Robertson Jr., James I. and Kunstler, Mort; The Confederate Spirit, Rutledge Hill Press, Nashville, TN; 2000.

Rowland, Dunbar; Howell, H. Grady Jr.; Military History of Mississippi 1803-1898; Chickasaw Bayou Press; Madison, MS; 2003.

S

Sifakis, Stewart; Compendium of the Confederate Armies—Mississippi; Facts on File, Inc.; New York, NY; 1995.

Sword, Wiley; Embrace an Angry Wind (The Confederacy's Last Hurrah); The General's Books, Columbus, OH; 1994.

T

Tucker, Glenn; Chickamauga: Bloody Battles of the West, Morningside Press, 1976.

U

Unit Muster Book: Records of Company A, 26th Mississippi Infantry, C.S.A., from 19 August 1861, to 25 March 1865; Official Records, OAG State Mississippi, Jackson, MS; 1865.

V

W

War of the Rebellion: Official Records of the Union and Confederate Armies. Published by the War Department, Washington, D.C.: 1881-1900.

Warner, Ezra J.; General's in Gray, Louisiana State University Press, Baton Rough, LA; 1987.

Wiley, Bell I. and Milhollen, Hist; The Embattled Confederates, Harper & Roe Company, New York, NY; 1964.

Woodworth, Steven E. and Winkle, Kenneth J.; Foreword by McPherson, James M.; Atlas of the Civil War, Oxford University Press, New York, NY; 2004.

X-Y-Z

27th Mississippi Infantry Regiment, CSA

COPYRIGHT ACKNOWLEDGEMENTS

Reprinted with the permission of the following sources:

25. Table 8 Pages 85 – OB CSA Bentonville NC: ibid.

26. CHAP XIII, XIV, XV, XVI: MS State Archives, Jackson, MS 1867 & National Archives, Wash., DC 1935

27. Roster 1 Pages 101-105 – Officers & NCOs: The National Park Service, Wash., DC 2005

28. Roster 2 Pages 106-161 - 27th MS Regt Muster Rolls: ibid.

29. Map 13 Page 172 – The Railways of the CSA: LC

ABOUT THE AUTHOR

Colonel Charles W.L. Hall, Ph.D. is an Educator, Psychologist and Minister and a longtime resident of Mississippi; a Confederate Historian, by being a practical student of the War for Southern Independence for over fifty years. His Great-grandfather an officer of the 46th North Carolina Infantry Regiment; Himself, past commander of Camp #1329, SCV; and awarded the War Service Cross by the UDC; and the Southern Cross by the OSC, for his preservation efforts on the Franklin Battlefield Restoration. COL Hall, a career officer of the U.S. Army's Adjutant General Corps, and a war veteran of the Cold War, Vietnam War and the Gulf War – retiring with over thirty years service. He has used both his academic training and military experience to bring this Confederate Regiment back to life. A.A.G.

A History of the
27ᵀᴴ MISSISSIPPI INFANTRY, CSA

Over 2,000 men were recruited for this regiment from the counties of Covington, Jackson, Jasper, Jones, Lincoln, Leake, Monroe, Perry, Oktibbeha, and Simpson, throughout 1861-1865! The 27th Mississippi persevered over three years of unbelievable hardship—valorously, and under the constant threat of death! Honoring all Mississippians past and present! Part of the real life story is given to us, through the memoirs and diary of 1st Sergeant Robert Amos Jarman, Company K "Enfield Rifles," Aberdeen, Monroe County.

Every attempt has been made to fully represent our regiment in this book, to include a Regimental Roster of all officers and men who selflessly served their state, their conscience and the Confederacy!

PLOWSHARES TO BAYONETS—27TH MS INF

_____"Limited Edition"_____

* * * PRE-PUBLICATION ORDER FORM * * *

Send to: _____ Ship by:

Address: _____USPS_

City/State/Zip: _____UPS_

Tel #: _____ Email: _____Other_

Payment Type: Check__ or Money Order__

Make Payable: COL Charles W.L. Hall

PLOWSHARES TO BAYONETS—27TH MS INF

_____"Limited Edition"_____

* * * PRE-PUBLICATION ORDER FORM * * *

Send to: _____ Ship by:

Address: _____USPS_

City/State/Zip: _____UPS_

Tel #: _____ Email: _____Other_

Payment Type: Check__ or Money Order__

Make Payable: COL Charles W.L. Hall

–

PLOWSHARES TO BAYONETS—27TH MS INF

_____"Limited Edition"_____

* * * PRE-PUBLICATION ORDER FORM * * *

Send to: _____ Ship by:

Address: _____USPS_

City/State/Zip: _____UPS_

Tel #: _____ Email: _____Other_

Payment Type: Check__ or Money Order__

Make Payable: COL Charles W.L. Hall

THE RAILROADS OF THE CONFEDERATE STATES, 1861

1. Baltimore & Ohio
2. Alexandria, Loudoun & Hampshire
3. Orange & Alexandria
4. Winchester & Potomac
5. Virginia Central
6. Richmond, Fredericksburg & Potomac
7. Richmond & York River
8. Richmond & Petersburg
9. Richmond & Danville
10. South Side
11. Norfolk & Petersburg
12. Petersburg R. R.
13. Seaboard & Roanoke
14. Virginia & Tennessee
15. Piedmont R. R.
16. Raleigh & Gaston
17. Roanoke Valley
18. Wilmington & Weldon
19. Atlantic & North Carolina
20. North Carolina
21. Western North Carolina
22. Western R. R.
23. Atlantic, Tennessee & Ohio
24. Wilmington, Charlotte & Rutherford
25. Wilmington & Manchester
26. Cheraw & Darlington
27. Charlotte & South Carolina
28. King's Mountain
29. South Carolina R. R.
30. Greenville & Columbia
31. Spartanburg & Union
32. Laurens R. R.
33. Blue Ridge R. R.
34. Northeastern
35. Charleston & Savannah
36. Georgia R. R.
37. Augusta & Milledgeville
38. Western & Atlantic
39. Etowah R. R.
40. Rome R. R.
41. Central R. R. of Georgia
42. Macon & Western
43. Upson County
44. Macon & Brunswick
45. Southwestern R. R.
46. Muscogee R. R.
47. Augusta & Savannah
48. Savannah, Albany & Gulf
49. Atlantic & Gulf
50. Brunswick & Florida
51. Atlanta & West Point
52. Florida, Atlantic & Gulf Central
53. Florida R. R.
54. Pensacola & Georgia
55. Tallahassee R. R.
56. Alabama & Florida R. R. of Fla.
57. Alabama & Florida R. R. of Ala.
58. Montgomery & Eufaula
59. Montgomery & West Point
60. Tuskegee R. R.
61. Mobile & Girard
62. Mobile & Great Northern
63. Spring Hill R. R.
64. Mobile & Ohio
65. Mississippi, Gainesville & Tuscaloosa
66. Memphis & Charleston
67. Wills Valley
68. Nashville & Chattanooga
69. Winchester & Alabama
70. McMinnville & Manchester
71. Tennessee & Alabama
72. Nashville & Northwestern
73. Louisville & Nashville
74. Memphis, Clarksville & Louisville
75. Edgefield & Kentucky
76. East Tennessee & Georgia
77. East Tennessee & Virginia
78. Knoxville & Kentucky
79. Rogersville & Jefferson
80. Memphis & Ohio
81. Northeast & Southwest
82. Alabama & Mississippi Rivers
83. Cahaba, Marion & Greensboro
84. New Orleans & Ohio
85. Mississippi Central
86. Mississippi & Tennessee
87. Memphis & Little Rock
88. New Orleans, Jackson & Great Northern
89. Southern R. R. of Mississippi
90. Raymond R. R.
91. Jefferson & Lake Pontchartrain
92. Pontchartrain R. R.
93. Mexican Gulf R. R.
94. New Orleans, Opelousas & Great Western
95. West Feliciana R. R.
96. Clinton & Port Hudson
97. Baton Rouge, Grosse Tete & Opelousas
98. Vicksburg, Shreveport & Texas
99. Alexandria & Cheneyville
100. Texas & New Orleans
101. Eastern Texas R. R.
102. Buffalo Bayou, Brazos & Colorado
103. Houston Tap & Brazoria
104. Galveston, Houston & Henderson
105. Houston & Texas Central
106. Washington County R. R.
107. San Antonio & Mexican Gulf
108. Memphis, El Paso & Pacific
109. Southern Pacific
110. Manassas Gap
111. Alabama & Tennessee Rivers
112. Hungary Branch
113. Grand Gulf & Port Gibson

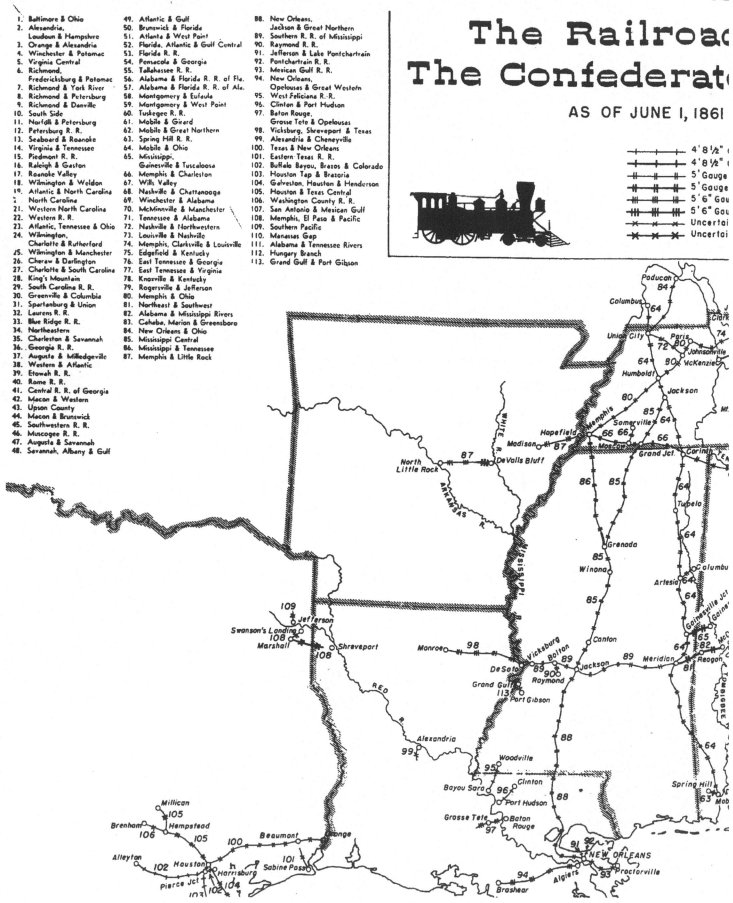

The Railroads of The Confederate States AS OF JUNE 1, 1861

4' 8½"
4' 8½"
5' Gauge
5' Gauge
5' 6" Gauge
5' 6" Gauge
Uncertain
Uncertain

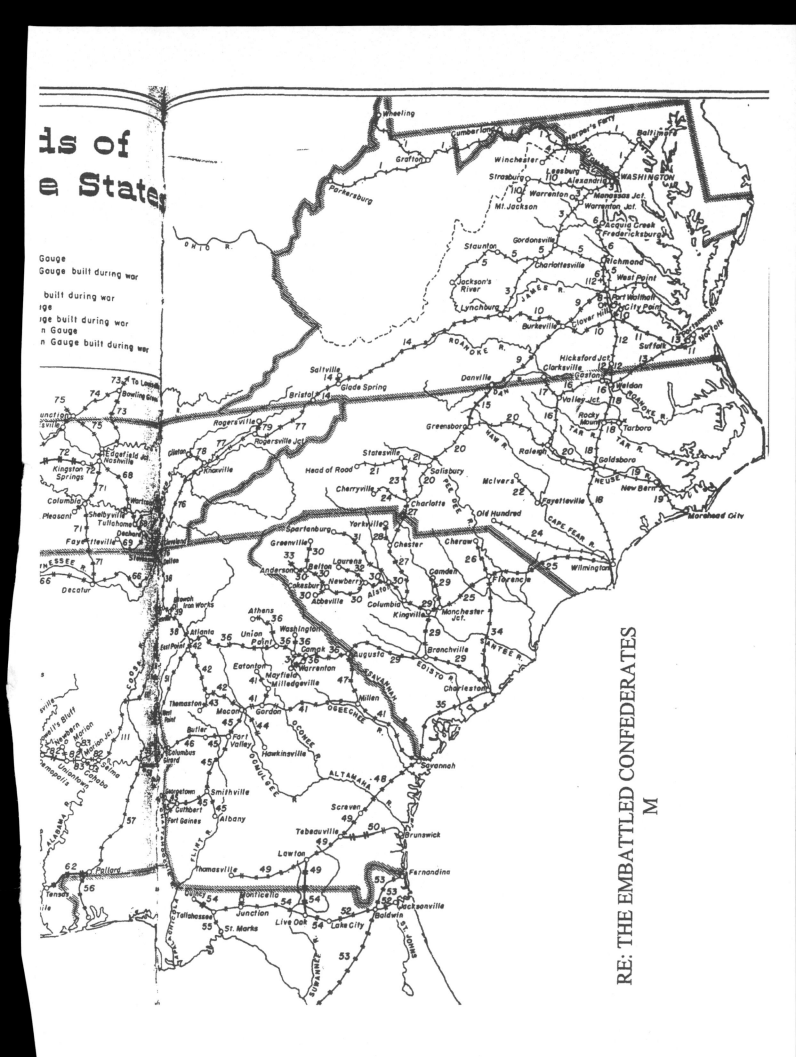

ds of
e States

Gauge
Gauge built during war

built during war
ge
ge built during war
n Gauge
n Gauge built during war

RE: THE EMBATTLED CONFEDERATES

M